The Year Was 1892

The story of the
Palmer-Donnell House

On the campus of
Blue Mountain College
Blue Mountain, Mississippi

A project of the
Palmer-Donnell House Guild
2021 - 2022

Lea Smith Bennett

CONTRIBUTORS
Charlotte Bryant Madison
Anna Jackson Quinn
Kathie Wessels Wilson

Book proceeds help fund the Palmer-Donnell House Endowment

DEDICATION

In memory of **Dr. Bobby P. Martin** – a genuine community leader in Tippah County and the state of Mississippi. He was a Trustee and generous friend of Blue Mountain College. He offered great encouragement to the first meeting of the Palmer-Donnell House Guild on April 24, 2018, bringing to the floor a recommendation for commissioning a written history of this house and family, offering his financial support in the endeavor.

In honor of **Dr. Bettye R. Coward**, President Emerita – the one to whom the Lord was pleased to give a vision for the Palmer-Donnell House and its potential. While serving as seventh president, she developed the initial plan for the renovation, secured funding for the purchase, and formed a team which would move forward the undertaking. Her account is included in Chapter 7. Tom and Bettye Coward continue as encouragers and supporters of BMC.

CONTENTS

FOREWORD

Anyone giving directions to Blue Mountain College is likely to advise visitors to our beautiful campus to look for the stately Victorian home that stands proudly just to the right of the Euzelian Gate, where generations of students have entered to grow in wisdom and departed to thrive in service to the community and to the Kingdom. Now known as the Palmer-Donnell House, this exquisite homeplace serves as a landmark, assuring watchful guests that they have arrived at the right place.

The year was 1892 when the beacon rays emanating from this sweet structure combined with those of the College to signal a warm welcome to many a weary traveler and to many an eager student in search of the light upon the hill. A few years younger than the institution founded in 1873 and first called Blue Mountain Female Institute, the Palmer-Donnell House is to warmth and hospitality what the College is to academic excellence, intellectual integrity, civility, and character. Together, they make great neighbors.

I invite you to immerse yourself in the history of this delightful home told from the perspective of one of its most colorful and engaging residents, the charming Lottie Palmer Donnell. I have no doubt that you will quickly find yourself right at home and will soon feel like a member of the family, just like so many others who accepted the invitation to "sit a spell" on Miss Lottie's porch.

On behalf of Blue Mountain College, I extend much gratitude to all who have endeavored tirelessly to restore the Palmer-Donnell House to its former glory.

The publication of *The Year Was 1892* – a book about a landmark – coincides with a landmark moment in the history of the College, the introduction of a new name, affording another shared celebration by these two long-time neighbors: The Palmer-Donnell House and *Blue Mountain Christian University*.

Soli Deo Gloria!

Dr. Barbara C. McMillin
President
Blue Mountain Christian University

PREFACE

Most likely it was Dr. Bobby P. Martin who planted the seed for this book project back in 2018. The Lord watered and nurtured that seed in my spirit until it was a driving thought, sprouting ideas daily. Now He has been pleased to bring to fruition this work – a telling of stories scattered through four generations of a happy, close-knit family. Stories which speak of the College and community that influenced the family's days, and which were, in turn, influenced by them. All the while the Lord orchestrated the rescue of a dear old house on the brink of ruin. He was also pleased to do all this through a small team of friends, a myriad of volunteers, and a network of advisors and supporters.

While I served as the voice of the book – Miss Lottie, a narrator-storyteller, and resident of the house over 62 years – it was the squad behind the voice that made this book a reality, using their creativity, their editing, teaching, managing, decision-making, and communicating skills to make this book what it is. *They are...*

> **Charlotte Bryant Madison** – this woman is our **Lydia.** Always learning, traveling, creating, Charlotte only began to dabble in photography after her retirement and created another career. Lydia was recognized for her impeccable taste, artistic creativity, and energy, which perfectly describes Charlotte, photographer, photo editor and text contributor.

> **Anna Jackson Quinn** – like **Anna** in the gospel of Luke, she is thorough, patient, kind, task-oriented, and totally dedicated to her objectives and aspirations. She has made a wonderful, helpful, encouraging, organizing, ever teaching, and always aiding lead editor and text contributor.

> **Kathie Wessels Wilson** – it was her bold, confident leadership that made her the perfect project manager, publishing administrator, and text contributor. She was our **Esther,** unafraid to take on a challenge and willing to use all her natural gifts and learned skills (and they are many) to make it happen.

My prayer for this little tome is that it would bless us all – writers and readers – to see that every story from yesterday furthers understanding and joy for living today; and that to keep history we must invest in it.

Lea Smith Bennett

We introduce our book in four paragraphs, written by the **Palmer-Donnell House Guild** officers – the writing project team members, all of whom are graduates of Blue Mountain College. Each expresses her personal motivation and expectation for this venture – a labor of love.

Lea Bennett, Class of 1974, Guild Secretary

"If these walls could talk." We have all heard the expression. It is used for saying that many interesting things have happened here, although we do not know the details. I recall a song sung by a popular performer several years ago that had a lyric something like this: "These walls keep a secret that only we know; but how long can they keep it?" Becoming passionately involved in the Palmer-Donnell House project many years ago, there was always in the back of my mind a desire to learn and share "details" sheltered in the walls of that sweet old house. Another line in the song I mentioned was "Can you keep a secret?" Well, frankly, no. Not any longer. Stories of faithfulness, family love, community friendships, and devotion to God and mankind have filled this little book – just a tiny few of the "details" and "secrets" that have now come to light. Enjoy.

Charlotte Madison, Class of 1969, Guild Publicity Chair

As a student at Blue Mountain College from 1965-69, I often dreamed about what it would be like to live in that precious little Victorian house at the entrance to the College. Much later in life, in 2012, I had the opportunity to reconnect with the house when members of my church (Mount Zion Baptist in Huntsville, Alabama) responded so graciously to the request for construction work on the BMC campus. Before it was the Palmer-Donnell House, those volunteers lovingly called it "the old Victorian house." After teams had traveled from Huntsville to Blue Mountain for five years, they completed their part of the renovation effort and others took over. But my part was not over yet! The Palmer-Donnell House Guild was formed, and I became an officer, serving alongside three women who have a passion for preserving, not only the House, but also the story of those who lived in it and those who served the College and community. In *The Year Was 1892*, Allie Palmer says: "Take care of my home." It has been my joy to work with the writing team in bringing to you readers the story of the house Charles and Allie Palmer built for their family, their descendants, and – unknown to them – a growing community of people who love history and Blue Mountain. I am thankful to have helped "take care of" the Palmer-Donnell home.

Anna Quinn, Class of 1961, Guild Treasurer

For many years I have been aware of the beautiful Palmer-Donnell House sitting at the entrance to our lovely Blue Mountain College campus. When I arrived on the campus as a student in the late fifties and early sixties, some members of the family were still residing there, and Miss Lottie was still coming to campus to work as treasurer for the Alumni Association in the College Business Office. When I returned as a faculty member in the nineties, the family was gone, and the house had fallen into disrepair. Upon retirement from teaching, I was able to participate as an officer in the Blue Mountain College Alumni Association and be a part of the renovation process when the College was able to purchase the house through some generous donations. Being here for the return of the house to again become a beautiful part of the Blue Mountain College campus as a welcome center and alumni house is a dream come true for me.

Kathie Wilson, Class of 1969, Guild President

I remember the old, yet pristine, white house east of the campus when I was a student at Blue Mountain College in the 1960s. I knew it was the home of Miss Lottie Donnell, and I even met her once. Life took me away for many years, and by the time I reconnected with Blue Mountain, the old home was a wreck. I was embarrassed and saddened. Yet, that stalwart group from Mount Zion Baptist Church in Huntsville, began work to save her anyway. Not long after, I was asked to co-chair, with my friend and classmate Charlotte Madison (also of Mount Zion), the committee to guide the renovation. While a daunting task, it seemed the least I could do to help with the 1892 house – one of the last truly historic structures remaining on campus. We had already lost Lowrey and Hearn-Jennings in my generation. We simply couldn't lose this landmark, too. Through the generosity of many, many people, we didn't. I'm thrilled the Palmer-Donnell House stands today, furnished with period and family pieces, for use well into the future.

ACKNOWLEDGMENTS

Special thanks to an invaluable Palmer-Donnell House Guild member and grafted-in writing project team member, **Renelda Pharr Owen**, Blue Mountain College Class 1978. A true writing project consultant extraordinaire, her shared life experiences, along with teaching, writing, and publishing savvy have been priceless.

Fond appreciation to special friend **Dr. Jody Hill**, President, Memphis Theological Seminary, former Blue Mountain College Vice President of Community Relations, and author of *38: the Chucky Mullins Effect*, New York Times "Best Seller Sports Book." Sir, you gave us great encouragement in the earliest days of this project.

Dr. Barbara Childers McMillin, Blue Mountain College President, and brave leader who didn't flinch one time when this penniless book project was proposed, whose constant encouragement and consistent confidence have been like a light shining on a hill – deepest appreciation, Chief.

The Estate of **Dorothy Christian** and its Personal Representative, her brother **Ed Wilson** (husband of Kathie Wessels Wilson) – by their generous gift to the Palmer-Donnell House Guild and its work, our project was no longer "penniless," and we had a running start for the challenging endeavor to endow the house.

The **Archives** of Guyton Library at Blue Mountain College through the assistance of **Shelby Carmichael** and **Dr. Tom Cockrell** generously provided most of the old photographs throughout this book, along with snapshots from family members. Most of the contemporary photographs were taken by **Charlotte Bryant Madison**.

CHAPTER 1

DO COME IN

Do not be forgetful of hospitality, for through this,
some have entertained angels unawares.
Hebrews 13:2
Berean Literal Bible

"Come on up here on this porch and tell us some good news." That's what Mama would say, as she waved at neighbors; and she even waved

Palmer House, circa 1892

to strangers, passing by on their way to or from town. Our house is beautiful for situation (Psalm 48:2 The Bible, King James Version) –

facing south here on Main Street in Blue Mountain, Mississippi, with Blue Mountain College to the west side and the railroad track to the east. We see many folks pass on their way to the College, our nearest neighbor.

Have you time to pause and visit a while? Good! My name is Charlotte Fredericka Palmer Donnell. Please call me Miss Lottie; at this stage of my life 'most everyone does.

Miss Lottie, circa 1935

Yes, this is an old house. It has stood here for over 125 years. You will find it furnished so nicely! It's decorated to suit its style, the Victorian period. Many friends and descendants took an interest in the project to restore this house; how I marvel at their generosity. I'll be sharing that story with you in this book. Yes, when I lived here as a child and then as a wife and mother, we had simpler, more practical furnishings and very little of the finery you will see here now. I suppose I should start at the beginning for you to get the full picture.

You see, at one time this land where the house sits, as well as that of the College, was part of a large farm called Prospect Hill, which belonged to Frederick Brougher, my papa's maternal grandfather. You will learn more about Colonel Brougher and his 1836 migration to Mississippi from North Carolina a little later.

2

My papa Charles Frederick Palmer had this house built in 1892. We moved here in the fall of that year when I was only three years old. Up until then, we had been living on the Randolph Palmer home place, just up the road a way toward Ripley with my paternal grandparents – Caroline Christine "Carrie" Brougher and Captain John Dederick Palmer. Their courtship is an interesting story. We won't forget to talk about that later.

Our family was deeply connected to that school and the community that was built up around it by General Mark Perrin Lowrey, founder of the College. He chartered both the College and the town of Blue

Charles F. Palmer, circa 1892

Mountain at the very same time according to the official record book ("Laws of the State of Mississippi 1877," page 250). On September 12, 1873, Blue Mountain Female Institute opened its doors and Alice Matilda

Palmer Family: Charles, Lottie and Allie, circa 1899

Cossitt sat in the primary class. Allie, as she was called, was my mother and would finish there in 1881 as the only member of that first graduating class of what had become Blue Mountain Female College. You can see her beautiful graduation doll in the historic doll collection at Guyton

Lottie and Jane Ellison Cossitt, her maternal grandmother, circa 1899

Library up on the campus. But we can walk up that way later on, maybe in another chapter. Now, back to my family …

In 1885, Allie and Charles, my mama and papa, married. Papa owned and operated a general merchandise store located right over there on the east side of Railroad Avenue at the corner. He and Mama had a little girl, Katie, who died as

a small child; I was born that same year, just a few months after her death. I followed in Mama's footsteps, spending all my school years right up there on The Hill, graduating in 1912 from what had become Blue Mountain College. I secured a position teaching art in the public school in Collins, Mississippi. In October 1914, I married Alonzo McWilliams Donnell and we lived on his beautiful farm near Baton Rouge, Louisiana. We had been there for only four short years when my father's health began to fail; so, we decided to return to Mississippi and this house to

Lon Donnell, circa 1920

help in the family business and to support Mama with his care.

Would you believe our connection to the College would grow even stronger? Alonzo, or Lon as he liked to be called, joined the faculty as the chemistry professor and later became chairman of the Department of Natural Science, serving the College for 40 years. And of course, I was involved with the Alumnae Association. It was my joy to serve as the treasurer for 45 years. That current keeper of all things historic over there in our Guyton Library Archives, Dr. Tom Cockrell, says that he came upon my old trunk and discovered thousands of letters. He salvaged some 700 of them for the Archives. He loves finding hidden treasures and working to clean them up, saving relics of antiquity. That man is the most organized packrat I have ever seen!

Well, as I was saying, this home would serve two more generations; Lon and I raised two daughters and two sons in this very house. Our oldest Alonzo McWilliams Donnell, Jr., whom we called Mac, was one of the first male graduates of the College in 1937; first daughter Marjorie graduated in 1947; then Alice, our youngest, in 1953. Our younger son, George, finished at Mississippi College. During the summers he worked in the BMC accounting office. He loved Blue Mountain College but thought he would allow Marjorie to be the only Donnell student at BMC at that time. Being a grateful (and too often, a proud) mother, I'll be telling you more about our children later. *Editor's Note:* Also see Appendix 1, *Descendants of Lon and Lottie Donnell*

George, Mac and Marjorie, circa 1927

I suppose you can see why there is in my heart such a fondness for this wonderful place. Here is where Lon and I enjoyed a rich, yet simple life together, endeavoring to serve others by the example set by our Lord and Savior. We were very active in our beloved Lowrey Memorial Baptist Church. Lon even followed in my father's footsteps serving as the Clerk of that church for ever so many years. I can just picture Lon now diligently completing and filing the large notecards for new members the very day of their baptism.

The cards were the modern system that was used along with the heavy, grey and brown ledger where the signature of each member was affixed with the date. These membership cards were carefully arranged in alphabetical order in a handmade, wooden box in the church office, long before there were computers and data forms to be completed and filed.

Mama, Lon, and I, and four children lived together happily in this house until 1955, when she left this old low ground of sin and sorrow to join Papa in heaven. We folded her empty tent and placed it beside Papa's up there in Blue Mountain Cemetery, to the west of here, along the ridge of this mountain. I missed her every day. She was the "house manager" here you might say. She kept us all in order. She loved to cook and serve meals for her big family. She loved her gardens, the vegetables, and the yard full of fragrant flowers, too. My children enjoyed gardening with her. Years ago, you would find a labyrinth of brick walkways throughout her gardens. My sons, Mac and George, laid them for their beloved grandmother, known to all as Miss Allie.

Our sons and daughters all married, of course, moved away, and had children of their own. We had 11 grandchildren! What exciting times those were, especially when they came back for visits. It was always a thrill to see them. How those grandchildren loved the train, just as their parents had in their youth. With the train station just right there across the street, from this porch we could eye every stop *The Rebel* made there. (You will learn about *The Rebel* and *The Doodlebug* passenger trains in another chapter.) Yes, I have to say it's true: all three generations could be seen, in their time, dashing out onto this porch at the sound of a train whistle, often calling out the familiar names of the engineers up front and the conductors in the caboose, to receive hearty greetings in return. I can even remember the simpler days in my childhood when the trainmen would alight from the caboose and chat with us briefly as our family and neighbors sat in the yard beneath the trees. The train would be stopped so the steam locomotive could take on water from the tower around that bend just north of the house. An abundant supply of water comes from numerous natural springs emanating from the hill lovingly called Blue Mountain. And yes, that name "Blue Mountain" begs yet another story, does it not? Patience, children, patience!

This old house witnessed the growth and changes of my own family as well as that of the College and the community. You see, General M.P.

Palmer -Donnell Family Home, circa 1925

Lowrey, his wife Miss Sarah, his daughters, Modena and Maggie, began the school in 1873. William Edwin (W.E.) Berry married Modena and became a partner in the family endeavor at the end of the third session. The Lowrey sons, too, began their educations there and would go on to be well prepared to join in the independent operation of the College for the first 47 years of its existence. Then in 1920 the Mississippi Baptist Convention assumed ownership. In 1956, just two years before my beloved Lon passed away, the College allowed men preparing for ministry to attend what had been an all-women's college. Now, that is an eventful part of the past which should be chronicled in another book.

As the years grew in number, I continued to live in this house until my health no longer allowed me to do so. In 1974, I moved to Texas to be close to Alice and Mac. After 87 years of being a part of the Blue Mountain College family, I had to leave. But I entrusted this sweet, old house to the Lord, asking Him to let her remain a sentinel at these gates; and I watched as He continued to pour out His blessings on my beloved Blue Mountain.

Well, I'm going to just insist you come on in from the porch. Let's sit in the parlor while you read on in this book to learn about the wonderful things that have happened through the years of my dear home's existence. You will meet, right here on these pages, many people – those who lived in this house, those who lived as neighbors and friends in this dual-community of college and town, and others who were here even as strangers and pilgrims, pausing to enjoy some Southern hospitality while they were passing through. You are ever so welcome to the Palmer-Donnell House.

CHAPTER 2

REMEMBER THE DAYS OF OLD

Remember the days of old, consider the years of many generations:
ask thy father, and he will shew thee; thy elders, and they will tell thee.
Deuteronomy 32:7
The Bible, King James Version

To study history is fascinating and really good for understanding the present and in preparing for the future, don't you think? In pondering the history of my house, I think of three outstanding mothers who shaped the story of this entire community. Long ago, among the old Baptists there was an expression of honor and respect given to women of quiet, yet effectual distinction. The term was "Mother in Israel." Actually a biblical expression, it comes from the story of Deborah, a prophetess and the only woman judge among the Israelites. The historical account is about God raising up two brave women to accomplish His work in defeating the enemy of Israel – Sisera, the Canaanite.[1]

Charles Spurgeon (1834-1892) died the very year this sweet old house was built. An English Particular Baptist preacher, he was known as the "Prince of Preachers." I can remember my father reading Spurgeon's sermons published by the *Baptist Record*. Well, Mr. Spurgeon pointed out rather succinctly how grateful he was for evangelical historians. They did not record "what worldly historians would write"; rather they recorded "just that which the worldly would have passed over ... What historian would have thought of recording the story of the widow and her two mites?" Spurgeon asked. And so it is that "Jesus values things, not by

9

their glare and glitter, but by their intrinsic value. He bids His historians store up, not the things which shall dazzle men, but those which shall instruct and teach them in His spirit. Christ values a matter, not by its exterior, but by the motive which dictated it, by the love which shines from it."[2]

I see three women who shaped the history of our home, the College, and ultimately the community of Blue Mountain as "Mothers in Israel." They were women God called to do that which He ordained and for which He perfectly fitted them. They were not women of the world or even women of which the world would ever take note; but they were valued, I am most certain, by Christ Jesus. How greatly His love did shine through them! Those three women are Sarah Holmes Lowrey, Modena Lowrey Berry, and Alice Matilda Cossitt Palmer.

SARAH HOLMES LOWREY
1827 - 1898

Sarah Holmes Lowrey
circa 1890

"If you are going to preach, don't be a half-way preacher. Go to your Bible and your books; I'll look after the farm and the children."[3] These were the very words of Sarah Raleigh Holmes Lowrey, the wife of then successful farmer, businessman, and brick mason, Mark Perrin Lowrey. Just three years after their marriage, Lowrey was called and ordained to the Baptist ministry at the age of 24. A passionate pastor and natural leader, he reluctantly agreed to accompany the fathers, brothers, and sons of families of his community, in what he believed would be a short-term period of defending his home state. He would go on to serve an extended period of honorable service in the Confederate Army, attaining the rank of brigadier general and would ultimately return to the war-torn South to establish Blue Mountain College right up there on that hill. Sarah was a practical, clear-headed woman throughout her life. Our very good friend, Professor David E. Guyton, our neighbor, and a colleague of my husband said that Sarah Holmes Lowrey "was a woman of character, courage, and rare common sense."[4] Sarah was born in South Carolina, in 1827 to Isham Holmes and Amelia "Millie" Ballinger Jones Holmes. In early childhood her family moved to Lincoln County, Tennessee. There, her father, mother, and she, along with her 14 siblings, enjoyed a prosperous country life. In 1848 adventure called them on west to Missouri and eventually Texas. Sarah chose to remain in Tennessee because she had already given her heart to Mark Perrin Lowrey and promised to become his bride. Being so close to my mama and papa, I could hardly imagine waving good-bye to my entire family loaded in wagons with all their belongings, knowing it was likely I might not ever see them again. But that is what Sarah did. It must have been God who gave her such courage.

So many things could be said about this woman of unimaginable strength. Those who knew her well regarded her as a woman of "quiet Christian graces, modest of demeanor, but firm of purpose, inflexible of will, and uncompromising in her fidelity to whatever she regarded as true and right."[5]

I must tell what the General, as he was respectfully called, or M.P. Lowrey, his usual signature, would declare to you this very day if he were here. "My Sarah," he would say, "is the one to whom most of my success in this life is due. She is a wise, unselfish, devoted wife and mother. By her fruits you may know her well. She is the mother of our eleven sons and daughters, as well as the sweet orphan girl, Mollie Hogan, who became our twelfth child. All these children attained places of

Mark Perrin Lowrey
circa 1874

distinction and service in this life. And according to the grace of God and the prayers of this truly loving mother, she saw them all come to know and serve their Savior."[6]

When in 1869 M.P. Lowrey purchased the Brougher house, out buildings, and large property, called "Prospect Hill," it was Sarah who set out to diligently transform the ante-bellum home of three stories into, not only the family residence, but also the first dormitory for the school which would open in 1873. She remained in a managerial role regarding the boarding and care of students for the first 25 years of the College. The institution owed much of its early success to her wise counsel, diligence in administration, and true servant's heart.

I must tell you a war story that Modena Lowrey Berry, would tell of her own childhood. Modena was Sarah and M.P Lowrey's oldest daughter and was not yet 12 years old when her father went away to war. In later years she would share many harrowing tales of the War Between the States during the story hours spent in the evenings with us girls of the school. She made history come to life in our minds. We would all gather in the main parlor of Lowrey dormitory where our beloved Mother Berry, as she came to be known, had her apartment. Sitting as close to her as we could, we always listened, totally enthralled with what she was sharing. One of my favorite stories went like this:

General Lowrey (at the time a colonel) had been wounded at the Battle of Perryville. With little chance of good nursing care, a leave of absence was granted so he might return home to recuperate until he could take his place at the head of his regiment once again. Within thirty miles of Kossuth, his home and family, he found it impossible to cross the picket lines of the hundreds of Northern soldiers who occupied Alcorn County. He ventured west traveling to his brother's home eight miles south of Ripley, Mississippi. After renting a crude cabin in a remote area near his brother, he would send for his family, cut off behind enemy lines in Kossuth.

Oh, what frightening days those were. "My mother was very brave," Mother Berry would say. "She was so determined to keep the farm and the family while my father was away." After the defeat at Shiloh in May 1862, the Confederates had evacuated to Corinth. Sarah Holmes Lowrey, the wife of a daring Confederate officer who had been known to elude the Yankees many times while infiltrating their forces, found herself behind the lines of the Union Army. On May 25, she had given birth to her second set of twin boys. The Yankees had harassed Sarah frequently, searching for her husband, raiding the farm for food, always trying to intimidate the children. Once they even stole the family cow. Later that same night, Sarah and son Willie made their way in the dark to the edge of the Yankee campsite. Calling softly to the gentle animal in a voice the cow knew well, they were able to steal her back!

"I remember one night," said Mother Berry, leaning in close, "I could see my mother dimly in the lamp light as she sat feeding the twins in her lap. The door burst open, and in came the Yankees to search yet another time for my father. Not finding him, they angrily emptied our larder completely, leaving mother without food for our family."

As a young girl I too sat sadly listening to Mother Berry's scary episode; I remember thinking: "How did they ever escape?" And that's the bravest story of all: About 10 o'clock one night in late October, the sound of a man's footsteps on the porch made hearts leap with fear. Yankee soldier! Then a voice outside the door said: "Sarah, Sarah, is that you?" Recognizing the voice, Sarah opened the door to her husband's brother. "Oh, Calvin!" she exclaimed. "What have you come for?" she implored, thinking of the danger for a Southern man coming within the Yankee lines. He quickly explained that her husband was wounded, was in Tippah County, and had sent Calvin to bring his family to him. Sarah, Calvin, and a neighbor woman slipped around quietly through the house, gathering up the meager clothes, to be packed in the ox-drawn wagon Calvin had brought and in the Lowrey family buggy. Young Modena and her sister Maggie were helping. By three in the morning, they were ready to move the children from the beds to the wagon and buggy. They put down a feather mattress in the wagon, then sheets, blankets, and quilts on top, along with seven children, most of them sound asleep, never waking during the hurried transfer.

Modena climbed into the buggy with her mother, the driver. Drawing the buggy up close behind Calvin in the wagon, with Modena holding in her arms one twin-baby, and Maggie sitting among the children on the bed in the wagon, holding the other twin, Sarah Lowrey looked back at her home for the last time. It took them until the late afternoon of the second day to reach Calvin's home 35 miles away. Just south of Ripley, Sarah spied her husband coming to meet them on his big war horse

Rebel. Calvin stopped the wagon as the older children piled out and ran to meet their father. He alighted from his horse and gave each of them a hearty hug with one arm while the other lay in a sling. Thanking Calvin, he looked up at Sarah, holding the twins now in her arms. Their eyes met; without words they shared a thankful, comfortingly warm smile.

Some weeks later, when his arm was healed and his family secure under the capable care of his wife, M.P. Lowrey called his family together as he was leaving once again to return to active duty. Standing in the stoop of the door, he opened his Bible and read Psalm 121:

I lift up my eyes to the hills.
From where does my help come?
My help comes from the Lord,
who made heaven and earth.

He will not let your foot be moved;
he who keeps you will not slumber.
Behold, he who keeps Israel
will neither slumber nor sleep.

The Lord is your keeper;
the Lord is your shade on your right hand.
The sun shall not strike you by day,
nor the moon by night.

The Lord will keep you from all evil;
he will keep your life.
The Lord will keep your going out and your coming in
from this time forth and forevermore.

The Bible, English Standard Version

Editor's Note: While M.P. Lowrey surely read from the King James Version, the College has adopted the English Standard Version for the College psalm.

Then, the General prayed a prayer of thanksgiving and supplication on their behalf and bade them farewell not to return for more than two years. Always faithful to write letters, he also sent money, the Confederate money which he was paid; but it would buy very little and grew more worthless every day. It is no wonder that the children of Sarah and M.P. Lowrey grew to be strong, independent people, all skillful, proficient leaders. During the war years, and afterward with many years as a traveling preacher, it was his wife, Sarah Holmes Lowrey, who kept the family safe and fed, running the farm efficiently.

For about 10 years before her death in 1898, Sarah Lowrey received a pension of $96 a year for services rendered by her late husband in the Mexican War. As I tell you of this last incident, you will see a clear indication of the woman's entire life and character. She reserved this pension strictly for benevolent purposes almost always done in secret – even her own children did not know until years later of many of her charitable deeds – including this one. The last eight years of her life were painful for her, and her activities were very limited after a fall which broke her hip and left her crippled. But her energy and enthusiasm for "doing the right thing" did not wane. During her last illness that saw her bedridden for four months, she learned of a farmer in the community who was critically ill and unable to gather his cotton crop. She sent for a young man she knew and hired him to do that job, using her pension money to pay him. So quietly was this arrangement made that no one outside of the young man and Sarah Lowrey knew these details until long after her death. Not only did her children and extended family appreciate and love her, but all in the community did indeed, "...rise up and call her blessed."[7] – a true Mother in Israel.

FRANCES MODENA LOWREY BERRY
1850 - 1942

Modena Lowrey Berry
circa 1920

It is very common in small communities for neighbors to borrow from each other – a cup of sugar, a sharp hoe, a postage stamp. Today I shall borrow again from our dear neighbor, David E. Guyton. He noted so clearly the truths that culminated in the life of Modena Lowrey Berry. I know he would neither begrudge nor be flattered by my "borrowing" his still true observations of Modena Lowrey Berry from his book *Mother Berry of Blue Mountain*. She was born in the middle of the 19th century (1850) and lived well into the 20th – remarkable. But to come to that milestone with one's full mental faculties and be able to "see in the lives of thousands the reflection" of one's "own ideals" was a rare privilege. This was the reality of Modena Lowrey Berry – "Mother Berry" to myriads of adoring daughters, life-long friends, and admiring acquaintances scattered all over the Mid-South and beyond. Hers was a life that beautifully blended the qualities of "purity, heroism, sacrifice, courage, gentleness, compassion, intelligence, and godliness."

Born in Alcorn County, Mississippi, in a comfortable and unpretentious frontier rural residence, she was the eldest child of M.P. and Sarah Holmes Lowrey. Modena had few dolls; she had no need. The rapid arrival of three little sisters, then a baby brother, followed by two sets of twin brothers gave Modena a natural maternal instinct that God would nurture and use all her life. She was puzzled to see, at the age of

11, the serious expression of her father and the hint of tears in her mother's eyes when the head of their household was called away by war. Ever certain that her father would do what was wise and right, she strove even harder to help her mother, meeting with determination and strength of character the double challenges placed on her young shoulders.

After the war years Modena took advantage of any schooling she could acquire in a state where no public school system had been restored. Following the example of her father, she was an ardent student of the Bible. She was grateful for the opportunity to study at Stonewall College

Stonewall College, circa 1869

in Ripley, Mississippi, which enhanced her natural love for learning and gave her a deeper appreciation for classical books. (See *Editor's Note* on Stonewall College at end of chapter)

Through the arrangements made by her father for her and her sister Maggie to complete the full course of study at Baptist Female College located in Pontotoc, Mississippi, Modena taught there half-time for two and a half years to cover their tuition and board. They both graduated in June 1873 and would be the first faculty members of the school in Blue Mountain founded by the Lowrey family later that same year. She would serve side by side with her father (who considered her his co-founder and named her the Lady Principal) for almost 12 years, until his premature death at the age of 56. She mentored and gave unwavering support to her brothers who then served as presidents – W.T. Lowrey and B.G. Lowrey. Then, from 1925 until her retirement in 1934, she continued to counsel, strengthen, and inspire administration, faculty, staff, and students as she gave faithful support to her nephew, Dr. Lawrence T. Lowrey, as he led the College. In Dr. David E. Guyton's words:

> Whether as Miss Modena, with the freshness of youth still upon her, or as Mrs. Berry, with her richer and riper wisdom, or as Mother Berry, softened, mellowed, and sweetened with the years, she was the heart and soul of the institution, which she served for sixty-one years, more than the life span of an average woman.
>
> Hers was the mother heart and she cherished her girls as her children.[8]

A tender love story will serve to illustrate well the devotion Modena Lowrey Berry always gave to whatever the Lord had called her to do. It was true that Modena was a romantic. She was a dear friend of my own

Modena Lowrey, circa 1876

beloved mother; we will speak more about that in the next section of this chapter. As was said of Modena: "Love was as native to her heart as laughter to her lips."[9] Just before the completion of her college work in 1873, she received a letter from William Edwin Berry, a young Baptist minister from Tippah County whom she had known for many years, as their families were friends. He was in school at Mississippi College with plans to go on to Southern Baptist Theological Seminary in South Carolina. In his letter he proposed marriage.

Locking the letter away in her trunk, she chose not to reply until speaking with her father. Modena shared how the talk went:

Late one night, when the rest of the family was in bed, I took Mr. Berry's letter to Father asking him for his counsel. He read the letter carefully, telling me what a high regard he had for Mr. Berry, but asking me not to get married until after we had established our school and had it permanently promoted. I promised Father I would do what he asked, for he told me that he would not even attempt to start the school unless I would stand by him in it.

Mr. Berry agreed and we became engaged. He continued his course at Mississippi College, graduating with first honors in 1875.[10]

W.E. Berry and Modena Lowrey were married on June 20, 1876, at the College auditorium with faculty, students, family, and friends in attendance. Mr. Berry purchased half interest in the school and served there on the faculty teaching Greek and Latin, and later as business manager for the growing school. He also served the community as a well-beloved pastor to rural churches. It was believed that he performed more baptisms, weddings, and burials than any other pastor of his era.[11]

W.E. Berry, circa 1876

Within three years the Berry family had begun to grow with the birth of a son, Mark Perrin Lowrey Berry, born in 1878. He was followed by daughter Clara Etta Berry born in 1883, and completing the rollcall for children was Joel Halbert Berry, born in 1889. But even after the Berry family seemed perfect in size, filling Berry Cottage (their home on the campus) with laughter and life abundant, there was room for more. Professor Berry's widowed mother and his sister lived with them. Later, when Joel was a small child, an aged and infirm lady called Grandma Callahan, known to few if any in our community, came to live at Berry Cottage. There, when not in her own comfortable room, she could be seen hobbling about on crutches, or sitting in her large chair by the fire, smoking an old clay pipe, reading the Bible. She would be lifted to church in a special chair by Lowrey Berry and some of his cousins; like a queen entering her court in triumph, she came rejoicing in the Lord. Grandma Callahan was fed, sheltered (at their own personal expense including her tobacco), and loved dearly by little Joel and all the rest of the family all the days of her life; and at the close of it she was sincerely mourned by her family of the heart.

Some years later Mrs. Berry took in an orphan girl who lost almost all her family to tuberculosis. The girl, whose name was Vance, enjoyed an affectionate fellowship with Clara Etta. With what was genuine fondness and devotion, Vance was mothered by Mrs. Berry, was educated at the school, married a fine young man, had a son, and in the tradition of the Berry children, was a contributing member of the community.

As the daughter of a Confederate brigadier general, with vivid recollections of the struggles of the South in the war years, Mrs. Berry was mindful of old Uncle Henry Mason. He was the only surviving Confederate Veteran in the area. For nearly forty years he served as the campus postman, taking the outgoing mail to the post office, and returning all the College mail to the campus for distribution. Even though she was nearing the end of her own life, she assumed responsibility for Uncle Henry after he had grown too deaf, blind, and feeble to carry out those duties. He was never neglected, and like poor Mephibosheth at King David's table, there was a place for this aged one at her table daily, enjoying her tender ministry and genuine concern.[12]

The young, the aged, the thriftless, the lonely, the forgotten were all touched by Modena Lowrey Berry's great heart of mercy. This selfless, godly, dynamic woman saw needs and met them. She was a woman all remember as Mother Berry of Blue Mountain, a woman who lived for generations in the hearts of many daughters, countless women really of untold generations, who took with them her spirit – the spirit of this Mother in Israel – and blessed others in so doing.

ALICE MATILDA COSSITT PALMER

1862 - 1955

Allie Cossitt Palmer
circa 1899

One of those "countless women" was my mother, known in our community as Miss Allie, and later to another generation as Grandmother Allie. Mama was one of two daughters born to Louis Pearl Cossitt and his wife Jane Ellison Cossitt, who had first migrated to West Tennessee and eventually to North Mississippi from Henry County, Tennessee. Young Allie was not quite 11 years old when she sat in the primary row of that white clapboard schoolhouse[13] among the 50

Replica of First School Building

students who marked the first day of Blue Mountain Female Institute on September 12, 1873. There stood two whom she idolized and who would be her treasured friends for a lifetime – Miss Modena Lowrey, who was almost 23, and Miss Maggie Lowrey, who was almost 21. My mother enjoyed all her years at the school – even the disappointment she endured on graduation day.

It was deep in the heart of Mark Perrin Lowrey to make the education that his school would offer an accessible opportunity to as many girls and young women as possible. Every girl, whether coming from a family of means or from a family of very limited means, was treated equally at the

1881

ALLIE COSSITT PALMER

Doll dressed and donated by
Lottie Palmer Dennie

Miss Allie's Doll in Guyton Library Collection

school. Any finery was forbidden; very simple dresses were the rule, with calico dresses as "special" to guard against any sense of financial inferiority among the girls.

In 1881, Miss Allie Cossitt was the only senior of that session. She had asked Miss Modena to permit her to vary from the calico rule since she would be the only graduate. Gaining permission, she made a beautiful dress for the occasion. When the General learned of the matter, he gently but firmly

overruled the special favor. Mother wore her calico to graduate all by herself. I remember well her speaking of her tearful disappointment but realizing in her heart General Lowrey's wisdom and being glad he was faithful to his convictions.

She was particularly happy when she and my father, Charles F. Palmer, built our home here, adjacent to the College. This is the very land that had belonged to his grandfather, you will remember. She loved my father's family, including his five brothers. She was close to my father's parents with whom they had lived the first few years of their marriage in the setting of a big, multi-generational family on the vast Randolph Palmer place. She enjoyed the entire

Palmer Brothers:
Seated Charles, John, Oliver
Standing Curley, David, Orlando, circa 1900

family and all the family stories, especially the one of how her father-in-law Captain John Dederick Palmer persuaded Caroline "Carrie" Christine Brougher to be his wife. A widower with five children, he told a somewhat fearful tale about his proposal to the lovely Carrie Brougher in 1858. His was just one of the uncountable stories lovers have shared through the years about "Love Rock," a huge stone jutting from the ground at the summit of Blue Mountain. Mama said that Captain Palmer would smile wryly and, likening himself to the legendary Indian brave and the maiden who spurned him, the Captain declared that he could not have won Miss Carrie's hand had he not proposed to her at Love Rock, where he hinted strongly that if she refused him, he would throw her headlong down the mountain. She was simply afraid to say "no."

How interwoven the lives of the Brougher, the Palmer, and the Cossitt families were! You see Miss Allie's father, my maternal grandfather Louis Pearl Cossitt, had pastored three churches in the area – Macedonia Baptist Church, Flat Rock Baptist Church, and Shady Grove Baptist Church from 1860 to 1904. He and General Lowrey were close friends. Like the General, my grandfather felt that young girls and young women of Baptist families should be educated by Baptists. My grandfather was very supportive of the establishment of the school,

23

sending both his daughters there. Indeed, it was important for young men to be educated, especially in the South where so much devastation still repressed the population. It was just as important for the minds and spirits of young women to be equipped and nurtured to help restore the region. Every nation is made up of communities, towns, and cities; these entities are made up of families; and families are born in the heart of a woman.

Allie Cossitt Palmer took her womanhood quite seriously. She made home a wonderfully warm and happy place. Her white-picketed yard was full of blooms, and her vegetable gardens abounded with plenty for the family she enjoyed serving at the table. She was a true matriarch of the family – never tiring of planning meals, managing the household, and supporting Lon and me as we endeavored to rear our children in the nurture and admonition of the Lord and fulfill our roles in the community and the College family. She always encouraged me in progressive but not foolish endeavors. In 1918 when we returned to Mississippi from Louisiana to help in the family business because my father had become ill, you remember, Mama and poor Papa were so happy to have our little toddler Mac in the house. Hearing a child's laughter made the duties of the caregiver lighter and the pains of the patient somewhat easier to bear. I loved my parents deeply and was grateful to be near them again. It was so sad that Papa died on Mac's third birthday, October 13, 1919.

Baby Mac Donnell, circa 1918

Mama rejoiced with us when each of our next three children were born – George in 1922, Marjorie in 1924, and Martha in 1932. "Martha?" you may ask. "I understood your youngest daughter was Alice." Now that is the perfect beginning of a story that is quite poignant to me, but will illustrate what a loving, industrious, strong, yet unobtrusive woman Allie Cossitt Palmer truly was. When our fourth child came, we did indeed name her Martha. Her almost eight-year-old sister simply adored

24

her and agreed with us that Martha sounded lovely when paired with Marjorie in conversation. It was not until a dear friend told me when Martha was quite young that my mother was deeply disappointed that we had named neither daughter after her. I was deeply hurt to think of having slighted my mother in that way. After talking with Lon, we brought the older children into our confidence and made a plan to correct the situation.

One evening while we all sat outside on the porch enjoying the lightning bugs sailing on a summer breeze and family chattering light-heartedly, I turned to Mama, who was holding the baby in her lap on the swing, and I said: "Mama, little Martha is so very much like you, in her smiling, sweet-natured ways. We have decided we will call her Alice Gayle from now on."

Mama could not hide her surprise, or her joy, and cuddled that precious baby girl in her arms saying softly, "Hello, Little Allie Gayle. It is so nice to meet you." The tears that she blinked from her eyes were met with mine when I silently and sincerely thanked the Lord for blessing us with this opportunity to bless my mama in this simple way.[14] Mama lived to see her "Little Allie Gayle" grow to become a beautiful young woman, a graduate of Blue Mountain College, and the bride-to-be of Captain Clarence Guelker of Ohio. We will talk more about Alice and her family, as well as her siblings later.

In my heart and mind Alice Matilda Cossitt Palmer will always be a true Mother in Israel, the one to whom I owed my brightest and fondest allegiance, and the one for whom I have been made to praise the Lord my entire life.

Look at me! We have finished this long second chapter of the book, and I have yet to bring you any refreshment. You just keep browsing, and I will get us some of Mother Berry's Tea Cakes.[15] They are fresh from the cookie tin and were one of my mama's staples in the kitchen pantry. I shall return.

Endnotes

[1] *Holy Bible*, Judges, Chapters 4 and 5.

[2] From *Spurgeon's Sermons*, Volume 6, Sermon #286: "Woman's Memorial", 1.

[3] From unpublished personal memoirs of General M. P. Lowrey.

[4] David E. Guyton, *Mother Berry of Blue Mountain* (Nashville: Broadman Press, 1942), 12.

[5] Ibid.

[6] Unpublished memoirs, Lowrey.

[7] *Holy Bible,* Proverbs 31:28a New King James Version.

[8] Guyton, *Mother Berry of Blue Mountain*, 55.

[9] Ibid., 41.

[10] Ibid., 41 & 42.

[11] Ibid., 45.

[12] Ibid., 73.

[13] A scaled replica of the original 24' x 36' school building, shown on page 21, is displayed in Guyton Library. This model was made by Allie Cossitt Palmer's nephew, Roger Mabry, son of Allie's sister Belle Cossitt Mabry who was also an early student of the school.

[14] Alice's name was legally changed from Martha Carney Donnell to Alice Gayle Donnell, thus giving her both her grandmothers' names.

[15] Mother Berry's Tea Cakes

8 cups plain flour	1 cup sour cream
1 cup Crisco®	2 teaspoons soda
1 cup oleo	1 teaspoon nutmeg
3 cups white sugar	Dash of lemon extract
3 whole hen eggs	

Mix soft oleo, Crisco®, sugar, eggs, sour cream, and lemon extract in mixer until very creamy. Combine soda with flour and mix well; gradually add flour mixture to creamed ingredients. This will be a heavy batter. Sprinkle flour over wax paper and roll out dough thin. Cut with cookie cutter and place on greased cookie sheets. Bake about 11 minutes at 375⁰, until light brown (darker on bottom). Take out of oven and loosen with a spatula. Let cool completely and store in airtight container.

Editor's Note on Stonewall College:

In 1866, the old school property on south Main Street in Ripley was leased to Mrs. M.J. Buchanan for 99 years; and she erected a large school building which opened as Stonewall College, a school for girls. Its early success was largely due to assistance from Mrs. Buchanan's brother-in law, Col. W.C. Falkner. The name of the school was almost certainly his idea in honor of Stonewall Jackson. The school had a large enrollment of local girls and boarding students. One of those students was Modena Lowrey who graduated in 1869 and became known nationally as Mother Berry of Blue Mountain College. The first building burned in 1883, and the property was turned over to Miss Harriett Winkler who had a large but not as pretentious building constructed. However, without Mrs. Buchanan the school lost much of its prestige and patronage. In the fall of 1886 "Old Stonewall" lost its identity by being merged with the Ripley Institute to form the Ripley Male and Female Academy.

Condensed from *HISTORY OF TIPPAH COUNTY* by Andrew Brown
https://www.msgw.org/tippah/ripley/ripleyedu.html

For further reading: *A Light on a Hill: A History of Blue Mountain College* by Robbie Neal Sumrall, Benson Publishing Company, 1947.

CHAPTER 3

AROUND YOUR TABLE

Your wife will bear children as a vine bears grapes,
your household lush as a vineyard,
The children around your table as fresh and
promising as young olive shoots.
Psalm 128:3
The Bible, The Message Version

The dining table: It is the universal gathering place. Meals are served there. Hospitality is celebrated there. Serious talks commence there. Birthday candles are ablaze there. Family stories are shared there. And long before funeral parlors and mortuary state rooms were the norm, oft times the deceased lay there as their bodies were solemnly washed and prepared for burial by their own families.

Sometimes that table is in a simple, country kitchen; sometimes it has a grandiose room of its own where "special" dinners are served on fine china and all are on their best behavior. But wherever "your table" is to be found, it is its own hub of the family, no

Palmer and Donnell family table restored 2021

29

doubt. That's how it was with the Donnell family. Our table was in the kitchen and was indeed, the center of daily life, so often, spilling over with friends, and friends of our children, laughing chatter permeating the whole house with joy.

Now there was a time when our table had its own room – the dining room. But when my father, Charles Palmer, grew very ill in 1918, he needed special care. So, the kitchen there on the northwest corner of the house was rearranged and the dining table was moved to the kitchen. Then, Mama and Papa's bed was set up in the dining room on the west side of the house, and Mama cared for Papa there the remainder of his life. When he passed, she kept the room for herself. Lon and I had a room upstairs. Our children were up there as well, until they grew old enough to move downstairs. This delighted my mama, as she was always close to the children. Having the boys there at her beck and call was something she relished. George loved to help her in the garden, keep coal brought in for the fireplaces, and tell her funny riddles to make her laugh. Mac was a good errand boy and brought her news from around town daily. When our girls grew older, like their brothers before them, they took the room downstairs, which is now the beautiful kitchen you see in the house with its wonderful eastern window aglow with morning sunshine.

The parlor was the front room on the southwest corner of the house. It was reserved for special guests, celebratory events, and for solemn occasions. There Mama's body lay in state with the sweet smell of roses from her garden and the gardens of many friends filling the house.

Parlor as first furnished for dedication
June 2019

Friends and family filed quietly by to express condolences and pay humble respect to a very beloved neighbor. Many years later when the house had been sold out of the family, one of the owners was a couple who had undertaken remodeling efforts. While they were asleep in the downstairs bedroom (Mama's room, and then mine after Lon died), they were awakened from their sound sleep by a lady standing at the foot of their bed. They described her as having white hair, which was pulled back in a bun. She said to them: "Please take care of my home." And then she was gone. They had never met or even seen photos of my mother, but they and many who heard their story were convinced it was Miss Allie, visiting the home that her beloved husband Charles had built for her in the year 1892.

Two wonderful things about the parlor were the Victrola and the piano. Our girls particularly enjoyed having their friends in, with permission, to entertain them in the parlor. While the family sitting room had the radio, such a marvel back in the 20s, providing enjoyable programming and news, the Victrola was an even greater source of amusement to the girls. They often listened to recordings of classical music and of some pre-selected and parent-approved modern music, such as Kate Smith's rendition of "God Bless America" and Tennessee Ernie Ford singing "Children, Go Where I Send Thee." They would sing along like a band of cherubs and then lose their parlor composure falling into fits of laughter trying to keep up with the fast-paced lyrics of Tennessee Ernie's song. They particularly enjoyed old recordings of Cal Stewart portraying "Uncle Josh" in his mythical town of Punkin' Center. My heart can still hear their giggles coming from that special room.

Inscription plate

The piano in the parlor belonged to my father's grandmother, wife of Francis Frederick Brougher. You will remember that I promised earlier to tell you about him. Now is a good time for that. F. Frederick Brougher had married a woman from one of the most prominent families of Philadelphia, Pennsylvania. Her name was Mary Ann

Christine Brougher's piano

Christine Stork. Colonel Frederick Brougher, as he was called, was of Austrian-Prussian descent, with European ancestors who came to the new world, settling in Delaware, New Jersey, and later Pennsylvania. Eventually Broughers made their way to the Southern settlements. In 1836 Frederick Brougher migrated with his wife and seven children from North Carolina to Alabama, then to Tippah County in North Mississippi. There he purchased a section of land (640 acres) recently ceded by the Indians, six miles southwest of the settlement of Ripley. The pioneer family pitched tents near the natural springs coming from one of the highest elevations in the state and built a four-room log cabin with a sleeping attic for the boys. The area would later be called Blue Mountain, and the natural water source would be called Brougher Springs. The cabin and tents would serve as living quarters during the seven years it took to build the home they had planned.

That piano of my great grandmother Christine Brougher, which I called my "most antique" antique, was brought by ox cart to Mississippi in 1842. Square in shape, the piano had a keyboard about two octaves shorter than the typical 88-note keyboard. When brought to the Brougher home, it was known as the first piano in the area built in Philadelphia and certainly, the only one bearing the inscription: "Made by E.N. Scherr, late Maker to their Majestys, the King and Princess of Denmark."[1]

The family tells a remarkable story of Christine's pioneer spirit. It seems that, in the earliest days of their arrival to the virtual wilderness of the former Indian territory, Mr. Brougher was stricken ill with a fever that lasted many weeks. With only Indians for neighbors and no doctor for many miles, Christine used her wits and knowledge of herbs found on the mountain to nurse her husband back to health. She also provided food for the family, using her husband's shotgun.

I got a little ahead of myself but do want to tell you more details about the construction of that beautiful home there by Brougher Springs. Well, at long last, with Frederick Brougher's health restored and temporary housing secured, the family and laborers began construction on what would prove to be a showplace of the region. Timber from the fertile woodland was cut with pit saws, bark was hewed off, and walls were constructed on brick footings. Those bricks, made from the clay soil so prevalent in North Mississippi, were molded and fired on site. The entire lower story was completely of brick; then the upper stories of logs and lumber were added. The house top was covered with handmade native cypress shingles.

Dunbar Rowland (1902-1937), attorney, archivist, historian, and first Director of Mississippi's Department of Archives and History, stated that the Fredrick Brougher home was the first brick house erected in Mississippi north of Jackson.[2] This home became the Lowrey residence and the first dormitory when the school was established in 1873.[3]

Early painting of Brougher home by T. Smith

The Brougher family moved into the home in 1843, but it was not fully completed for some years. Later, it was a most gracious setting for the wedding of the oldest daughter, Caroline Christine "Carrie" Brougher to Captain John Dederick Palmer. This celebration was only one event in the house's illustrious history of social prominence.[4] I wonder how many beautiful musical presentations rang through the antebellum home from that sweet old piano that later came to sit in our parlor for so long.

That dear piano and Victrola in our parlor gradually grew silent as the children got older, were more active in school and community life, completed educations, and then moved away to make families and lives of their own.

Mac, my eldest, was among the few men graduates of the College, which at the time, of course, was a women's college with an infrequent

**Lorrayne and Mac
circa 1947**

male student from administration and faculty families attending classes. He completed his work there in 1937 before going on to the University of Mississippi. Then World War II took him far from home and the family table as it did so many other mothers' sons. In 1942, he joined the Army Air Corps at the age of 25, received his pilot wings and transitioned into the B-17 Flying Fortress. He was assigned to the 8th Air Force in England with the 384th Bomb Group. Mac was on active duty from February 21, 1943, until June 1, 1946. He came back to Mississippi after the war and returned to the University of Mississippi to earn his master's degree. It was there that he met Lorrayne Vick through her roommate. It was the storybook tale of love at first sight. They married on December 21, 1947. The couple moved to Denver, Colorado, in 1948. Mac received his M.D. from the University of Colorado school of Medicine in June 1950 and then re-entered the U.S. Air Force. At the risk of sounding like a boastful mother, I have to tell you that Mac was one of only a few individuals at the time to serve with a dual rating of physician and pilot. He served his country for 30 years before retiring as a Colonel in 1974. Upon his retirement from the Air Force, Mac settled in Austin, Texas, and served as the Deputy Commissioner of Health for the Texas Department of Health from 1974 to 1984.

Oh, they had lived all over – Washington state, Colorado, Alabama, Virginia, Washington D.C. and finally, Texas. They had one sweet baby girl, Anne Gayle (called Gayle by us all), born in 1956, who grew up, married, and gave Mac and Lorrayne a beautiful granddaughter, Andrea Gayle. Mac's greatest joy in life was his "three girls": his wife, Lorrayne; his daughter, Gayle; and his granddaughter, Andrea. After Mac's death in 1995, Andrea gave birth to great-granddaughter, Elizabeth Gayle. Lorrayne died in 2019. Throughout their marriage, they were faithful to visit when they could. Lon and I were always appreciative of the dedication they gave to their work, their churches, and their communities.

Gayle likes to tell folks why she is so afraid of trains. It was a case of early childhood trauma. It seems that Mac and family were here visiting in one of those exciting times when more than one set of our children's families were here together – and our dining table was really full at mealtime! In summertime there was a ritual with our children and then the grandchildren after them. When they heard the long whistle of the train as the engine headed south around the bend about midnight, they would all jump up out of bed, dash out on the porch in their pajama tails and wave like crazy at the engineer and conductor. Well, it seems that without explanation, Mac grabbed toddler Gayle up out of a dead sleep, swept her outside in his arms, set her onto the wide porch railing amid all the clamor of the other children, and taking her little arm, he helped the bewildered little girl "wave" to the horrifically loud train with its glaring bright headlight. Oh, the memories…

George Frederick Donnell, our second son, was like his brother in that he too would know the life of a soldier in war time. George was at Mississippi College in Clinton when he enlisted in the army in 1942 but was allowed to finish his degree before reporting for service to Fort McClellan, Alabama. Proving himself to be an outstanding marksman, he served as a heavy machine gun instructor for a time before heading to Italy. He led an infantry squad through Rome, Pisa, and Florence before being wounded October 12, 1943. His right hand fragmented by a mortar round, he received treatment for weeks at aid stations and hospitals in Europe before finally boarding a hospital ship on Christmas Eve heading to the United States. He spent New Year's Eve in the harbor of Casablanca and reached

George and Arlene circa 1946

Boston January 10, 1944. George was treated at several locations, finally in Springfield, Missouri, at O'Reilly Hospital for his last surgery. There he met and fell in love with Arlene Compton, who was a doctor's secretary and young war widow. They married on Easter Sunday, April 21, 1946, after friends had told them for months they should "marry and raise a house full of Bob Hopes." That bespeaks their mutual sense of humor and joyful demeanor. As his bride, Arlene brought George a wonderful little son, Ronald, whom George lovingly adopted. The child had lost his father to the war. George always put me in mind of his father. Lon and he had such similar natures. Yes, father and son were very much alike, charming, and full of fun.

George and Arlene moved to Blue Mountain. George bought the movie theatre, and our first granddaughter came in 1949. But just a few years later the movie house burned, and they returned to Springfield to find work. There they remained and raised their family – Jan, her older brother Ron, and younger brothers Fred and Greg. After the move back to Springfield, where George had a 30-year career with the United States Postal Service, George and Arlene were faithful to visit here at least annually. Their children would come as often as possible, especially in summer when they knew some of their cousins would be here! Even now, I can see those cousins, who seemed as close as siblings, sitting with us on the front porch, enjoying lemonade, waving at the train, sneaking to put pennies on the track, hiding in the attic when it rained to hear the thunderous drops on the tin roof, following my mother in her greenhouse, picking up pecans under the trees, and persuading Mama to make a pie, piling up three and four in the bed on the sleeping porch counting down 'til midnight when the whole house would rattle as the train flew by.

And it was George who lived the longest of our children, dying at the age of 97 in September of 2019, leaving as his progeny eight grandchildren and 12 great grandchildren. And it was George's "best friend" that you shall meet next; born just over two years after him, his little sister – Marjorie Graham Donnell, our first daughter.

Now, how do I tell you about our Marjorie, her father's favorite tennis partner, and my first sweet little girl after enjoying two boys and 10 years of marriage? Marjorie's only daughter, Carol, now Mrs. Gary Reynolds, may have been challenged in elementary school, like so many children were in the 50s and early 60s, to write about why she loved her mother. If so, I can imagine just what fifth-grade Carol would have said.

Why I Love My Mother

My mother, Marjorie Donnell Easterly, was born in Mississippi. She graduated from Blue Mountain College, and then Louisiana State University. She is a speech and drama teacher. She tells great stories. One of my favorites is the one about her first job. It was at Union College in Barbourville, Kentucky. During the train ride on the way to Kentucky, she kept seeing a tall, slender lady walking up and down the aisle. The lady had her hair in rollers! My mother wondered why she would be seen in public like that. My mother, her mother, or her grandmother would never do that. Well, it turned out, the lady would be her boarding house roommate, and co-teacher at the college! They have been friends a long, long time now and still laugh about that day on the train.

Another funny thing about her first job was that many of her students were older than she was because they were men who had gone off to fight in World War II and were now back home wanting to finish school. She met one man like that on what they called a double date. He was nice. He loved to dance and travel and tell jokes. He owned a car dealership. They got married on August 21, 1950. He's my daddy and his name is Charles Thomas Easterly.

I think my parents love each other so much because they both love the Lord, and Mother is pretty. She is from the South and is smart and likes to take care of others, like my brothers and me. She likes to have company. She is such a good cook that sometimes Daddy calls home in the afternoon and says: "Hey, Honey, I'm bringing someone home for dinner." She does not even fuss, but just laughs and says: "Okay, I'll put some more water in the soup." Daddy calls her his Proverbs 31 wife.

When I was very little my mother quit working at her job at Cumberland College so she could play with us at home. We all liked to read together and listen to her stories about growing up in Blue Mountain, Mississippi. My favorite is the one when she and my Uncle George climbed up on a high ledge at the college where my grandfather was a professor. They squeezed around on the ledge to the window of his classroom where he was teaching chemistry and began to wave at him and his students. My grandfather was very surprised, and I think a little unhappy about that too, because his classroom was on the third floor of the building! He rushed over to the window, raised it quickly, and grabbed both of them, dragging them into his room and rushing them out into the hall. He sent them home after telling them in a very stern voice that they could expect to be punished later. I am not sure exactly what happened when he got home, but Mother said that she and Uncle George certainly did not hear him whistling and humming that afternoon as he usually did when he walked down the hill to their house on the corner. And she said they also did not ever climb on the ledge again.

Mother has been my brother Charles' homeroom mom before, so I got to go to the parties in his room too. I also have a little brother Stuart. When he was about six, we moved to Danville, Kentucky. Mother said it was good that Daddy would be taking a new car dealership there and that we would all be going to a big new school. We were excited, except our new house was very small. I missed our old house in Williamsburg. That's Kentucky too. But Mother said it would be easier to play hide and seek in that house and that we would be closer to Stuart's school and to the church, and that there was always something to be grateful for. We spend a lot of time at Lexington Avenue Baptist Church. Mother is always helping do something there. She goes to meetings, she teaches Sunday School, she even wrote a play about the church's history. She directed it and we got to be in it with some other kids and grownups too!

Whatever Mother does makes other people happy. She is always cooking something good to eat for us and for other people too. One time when she and Daddy were having friends over and everyone was talking and laughing, I sat on the couch next to a lady who was a friend of Mother's. She was a quiet lady, and I liked her smile. She said to me, "Your mother is one of my favorite people. She always makes me feel like I am the smartest person in the room."

Although we are supposed to talk about our mother's hobbies, I can't think of any hobbies that Mother has except she does like to read to us, and even to herself, not out loud of course. She likes *to be at church, and in the kitchen, and with Daddy when he goes on trips for work. Oh, she does like to go to the plays at the college. Sometimes she takes us! She really likes children. She said to me once: "Carol, I hope you, Charles, and Stuart have a lot of children that will come to see me and call me 'Grandmother.' I hope we do too. And when I have my children, I want them to love me just like I love my Mother.*

Marjorie and her family came every summer from Kentucky to visit.

Carol Easterly Reynolds, daughter of Marjorie Donnell Easterly, returned to the Palmer-Donnell House Grandfather Lon Donnell's eyeglasses, a memento treasured by her mother

Their arrivals were in the middle of the night, but they always found me sitting on the front porch, anxious to see their safe appearance and feel their warm hugs. The children loved finding some of their cousins here, too, quite often. They enjoyed looking in the window seat of the kitchen and finding "their" playthings. They kept busy – a happy little cache of cousins dragging metal toy trucks and tractors through the dirt under the trees or playing Parcheesi around the family table on rainy days. Adventurous as George and Marjorie had been, their offspring carried on the tradition. They once climbed up some boxcars parked on the railroad track spur. Carol, however, got half-way up and froze in terror. Crying out in a pitiful panic, she was soon rescued by one of her heroes – Uncle Mac. They would visit the drug store downtown as often as they could, drink cherry Cokes, and hear proprietors Garland and

Jewel Allison tell stories about Marjorie working there for them as a young lady. Carol often wanted to "sleep with Grandmother Allie," and watch her take down her silky white hair from its bun and brush it 100 strokes before reading from her Bible to Carol.

Marjorie, who died in 2007 at the age of 82, did indeed enjoy five happy, healthy grandchildren who loved her. They adored Marjorie, just as her children did, and just as her own mother and grandmother had adored her.

Our family was complete in God's providence with the birth of our second daughter June 21, 1932. "Little Allie," as my mother would often call her (you remember that story), was close to Mama. I would often walk home from the College and find them both in the garden. Mama, at almost 75, still enjoyed outdoor productivity, and her "shadow" – Little Allie, about five – followed her around striving to "help." The little helper carried Mama's basket while they filled

Photo by Ellen Guelker Scott, daughter of Alice Donnell Guelker, granddaughter of Lottie Palmer Donnell, Great-granddaughter of Allie Cossitt Palmer, and great-great granddaughter of Jane Ellison Cossitt, to whom the basket first belonged – making it now a fifth-generation basket

it with tomatoes, squash, okra, and, of course, some fresh flowers for the pleasure of those around our table for supper.

Alice, to family and friends, was a bright child who had her father's inquisitive spirit and thirst for knowledge. After finishing at Blue Mountain College in 1953, she went to Vanderbilt, earned her master's degree, and taught in Rome, Georgia, until her marriage to Captain Clarence William "Gil" Guelker in 1955. Alice happily assumed the role of army wife which, for the first 20 years of married life, led her to many locations. She even came back to Blue Mountain for about a year to make a home for her children while her husband was on a distant assignment. Also like her father, Alice was a natural teacher, serving churches as Sunday School teacher wherever she and Gil resided, including a 20-year stint with fifth graders at Hyde Park Baptist Church in Austin, Texas. An active volunteer in many organizations, Alice had the gift, not only of teaching, but also of leading. A renowned hostess, she was a devoted wife for over 50 years and loving mother to Mark, Ellen, and Elizabeth, who gave her eight grandchildren together. As I mentioned, Alice and her three small children had returned to Blue Mountain for a time, while Gil was stationed far away. Having them here was especially precious to me. Alice succumbed to Alzheimer's disease in 2007, after years of devoted care by Gil and her children.

Who was it that sat at the head of our table? The man who loved to walk with his children in the woods and point out the flora and fauna so abundant there. The man who would take endless turns at checkers and other board games to spend time with his children and later his grandchildren. The man who was the first-born of four sons, and who was yet a young boy when he lost his father, George Richardson Donnell. And would lose his mother to yellow fever just a few years later. His mother was Virginia Gayle McWilliams Donnell, a descendant of Thomas Gayle who fought in the Revolutionary War, and Peter Smith Gayle, who pastored churches in Nashville and other parts of Middle Tennessee. Yes, at the head of our table sat a man descended from Robert II, King of Scotland (1371-1390). A man who at birth had a Bible placed under his tiny hand so that it was the first thing in this world he touched.[5] He was the man who made me his bride in 1914 – Alonzo "Lon" McWilliams Donnell.

Lon Donnell
circa 1914

It is often said that "opposites attract" and that was certainly true of Lon and me. Lon was far more sociable than I was. He loved being outdoors far more than I did. He was the one who made friends quickly and "never met a stranger" as another saying goes. He could strike up a conversation with anyone and learn something from them that he invariably remembered.

He had been very devoted to his mother and worked hard to help her care for his younger siblings; he was a lad of only 12 when she died and left four young children as orphans. Following her death, the boys spent most of their years in boarding schools with summers in the homes of extended family. Lon was able to work and get a good education – completing his bachelor's degree at the University of Missouri, a master's degree in natural science from George Peabody College (now part of Vanderbilt University), and further graduate work at the University of Louisiana. In 1912, believing agriculture to be his profession in life, he bought a farm in Louisiana.

Even in the first four years of our marriage while we were living on his farm about 20 miles north of Baton Rouge, Louisiana, whenever his family needed him, he made every effort to help. One of his brothers even came to live with us while we were still enjoying our honeymoon.

Lon cared not only for his brothers, but for their families as well, even after relocating to Mississippi. He took advantage of an opportunity to go to see them annually during spring break at the College. He would volunteer to transport any of the girls from Louisiana to their homes for the week-long break and then go and visit with his family before returning with his riders to the campus at the end of the week. Thankfully, the parents of these girls were always grateful for having their daughters traveling with a trusted professor and not by public conveyance. They were faithful to compensate him for his gas expenses. The Lord always provides when one is willing to serve.

One of his favorites among his Louisiana kin was a niece, Gayle Donnell. She was his brother George's daughter; her father had died at the age of 41 from a bleeding stomach ulcer. Gayle was only two years old when she lost her father and had very little memory of him. I believe Lon was the closest thing she knew of a father as her mother and grandmother raised her. Lon and Gayle adored each other. She delighted in reminding us that she was born on our fifteenth wedding anniversary, which kind of made her a "twin" to our Marjorie who was born on our tenth anniversary. Gayle came often for visits, fitting in so nicely in age between Marjorie and Alice who both loved having her here. At their encouragement as well as mine and Lon's, Gayle attended Blue Mountain College for two years before returning to Louisiana and finishing at LSU because her mother needed her at home.

We all loved Gayle. I remember the night that she and Lon, who was a wonderful storyteller, had a touching little talk. She was not quite 10 years old when she said: "Uncle Lon, did you know that Grandmother Allie leaves a lamp on all night?"

"Yes, Gayle, I know," he answered calmly as they sat in the swing watching twilight begin to give way to opaque night.

"But why, Uncle Lon? Isn't the oil too expensive? Everyone says we are living in a depression. Why does she need the lamp?"

"Well, you see, Gayle, Aunt Lottie over there shelling those peas that you and Grandmother Allie gathered this afternoon was not exactly like you have always been — an only child. She was not the only little girl her mother and father had. Before Aunt Lottie was born, Grandmother Allie had another baby. Her name was Katie Lucille. She was born in 1887 and was a precious baby girl that Grandmother Allie adored. One night while little Katie Lucille was sleeping in her cradle, she became very ill, gasping and struggling for breath. Grandmother Allie and her husband Papa Charles were trying to light the lamp so they could get the baby up from the cradle and find out what was wrong. But sadly, so sadly, the lamp would not light and by the time they got to the baby, she was not breathing at all. She never took another breath. From that time on, Grandmother Allie has kept a night lamp burning, even while she slept, so that if anyone needed her, she would be able to get to them to help."

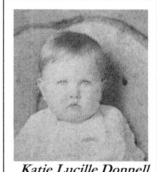

Katie Lucille Donnell
circa 1888

Gayle sat quietly for a good while; then she said: "I think I will go in and tell Grandmother Allie that I love her and bid her good-night." And she slipped off the swing and went inside quietly. Shortly, Lon came to my chair, smiled down at me, then reached to help me gather up the peas and bowls. Taking me by the arm, he led me inside. It was too dark to sit out any longer. How thankful I was for my husband, a father to more than just his own, a caring man who understood people's hearts.

43

Yes, in so many ways Lon and I were opposites. I preferred my quiet corner of the sitting room, working at my desk by the east window, keeping up with the vast correspondence[6] involved with the Blue Mountain College Alumnae Association – I was elected treasurer in 1929 and served until resigning in November of 1974, my health preventing my further service. My "business days" were good days of walking up the hill to the College business office to check the mail, collect, and record all dues and gifts received for the Alumnae Association and keep an accurate account of all transactions. Some days I went to Lowrey Church to prepare financial reports. When those duties were fulfilled, I came home to relieve Mama who managed the house and helped with our children. Too, there was the joy of finding a few minutes to relish inspiration from the beauty of Mama's garden and paint a small illustration. It might be a tiny bouquet on a lamp, or a single rose on a personal card to send to a dear friend like Mrs. May Gardner Black in Nashville, or a sleeping yellow kitten on some note to a neighbor feeling under the weather. Yes, my days were well-ordered, simple, and quiet for the most part.

But that Lon was always on the move – he would take the children to special programs presented at the College or high school. He would walk the girls to their play rehearsals, choir practices, up to the College pool to swim. He would take the boys with him whenever possible to perform any and every task of service to a neighbor, or community duty, such as serving as the town clerk for many years. What an example he was to the children and others around him! He found great joy in being a good citizen, in having an ever-willing spirit of kindness in servanthood, and in sharing his faith in subtle, meaningful ways, almost always whistling or humming a hymn as "he went about doing good." (Acts 10:36 The Bible, King James Version)

In 1946, the *Mountaineer*, Blue Mountain College's student annual, was dedicated to Lon. The students said so well what all knew and loved about my cherished Lon.

To Alonzo McWilliams Donnell, our chemistry professor, because of his constant friendliness and a never-failing sense of humor
- his high personal standards and ability to bring out our best
- his sincere understanding and tact in helping us solve our problems
- his warm and genuine interest in the little things that matter to us
- and most of all his Christ-like character,
we dedicate this, the 1946 *Mountaineer.*[7]

Now that you have met our family, I hope you will join me in the next chapter when we shall take one of Lon's walks and see what lies outside the picket fence surrounding our house. We want you to meet our neighbors and friends in the lovely little town called Blue Mountain. We will climb the hill and venture into the halls of academia at Blue Mountain College sitting sublimely above us – a light that truly "sends afar its beacon rays."[8] We will go back in time to ride the Rebel and the Doodlebug – remember, the depot is just across the street. I will be waiting here for you when you return for our walk to town.

Endnotes

[1] Fredrick Brougher Smith, personal writings, "Ancestral Family History" September 1980, 43.

[2] Smith, "Ancestral Family History," 42.

[3] Ibid.

[4] The Brougher home and later Lowrey home and first College dormitory was destroyed on February 17, 1900, when a devastating fire swept the campus causing widespread damage. Three buildings were totally destroyed by the blaze driven by raging winds and snowstorm – The Brougher residence, Boright Cottage, and another large dormitory built only five years earlier. A solemn assembly was called at daylight the next morning to fully account for all students. President B.G. Lowrey with an anxious heart, called the roll.

Seven girls were sick with the measles and had been hastily carried to safety during evacuation of the buildings. Finally, with every student and staff member fully accounted for, President Lowrey immediately knelt in prayer. An hour-long thanksgiving service commenced with attendees humbly praising the Lord for the mercy that had granted no lives to be lost. The President acknowledged that from its founding almost thirty years before, God had had His hand on the College. "He would not forsake us now," he said, "but will indeed bring good out of it all."

Reverend E. L. Wesson, of New Albany, whose daughter was a student, had come as soon as he received news of the fire; he attended the thanksgiving service. He stated: "I saw the ruins. I also saw the Christian spirit manifested by those who had suffered loss…Submission to God's will, confidence in His guidance, and re-consecration to His service was manifest on every face."

Robbie Neal Sumrall, *A Light on a Hill: A History of Blue Mountain College*. Nashville, Tennessee: The Benson Printing Company, 1947, 31 - 32.

[5] This is a family story corroborated by several. This same Bible was passed to Stuart Easterly (Marjorie's son, Alonzo's grandson) and Stuart's first son was guided to touch that Bible at birth.

[6] In June 2018 a large antique trunk was discovered in storage at Blue Mountain College. The trunk and contents – thousands of hand-written pieces of Lottie Palmer Donnell's business correspondence – were evaluated by Dr. Tom Cockrell, College Archivist, who restored what was not destroyed by mold and mildew. Only 20% of the documents could be salvaged, processed, and catalogued, which amounted to 745 letters dating from 1939-1970. They remain in the Archives, Guyton Library, Blue Mountain, Mississippi.

[7] Blue Mountain College, *Mountaineer,* 1946, Dedication page, Archives, Guyton Library, Blue Mountain, Mississippi.

[8] *Alma Mater* of Blue Mountain College, words by Susan B. Riley, music by Julia Lee Godwin Berry and Linda Berry.

CHAPTER 4

I AM THE LORD WHO BROUGHT YOU OUT

I am the Lord, who brought you out of Ur of the Chaldeans
to give you this land to take possession of it.
Genesis 15:7
The Bible, New International Version

"Did you know that on the very day General Lowrey chartered Blue Mountain Female Institute, he also chartered the Town of Blue Mountain?" Lon asked me one afternoon when he returned from City Hall where he had been doing his "clerking" as he used to say.

"Of course, I did," I answered. I had been a resident of Blue Mountain all my life and I loved its rich history. But Lon was what I call a perpetual student (I think the term now is life-learner – has a nice ring to it, doesn't it?). So, I knew he had been browsing through some of the very old record books learning all he could about the history of his community.

What a community it is. What a community planner the Lord had made of General M.P. Lowrey! He knew well that for the South to ever come back to her former glory she would have to be restored from her very grass roots – meaning that it was the common, ordinary people, not the elite aristocrats or even a political party who would rebuild and reunite our country. Those people would especially and most assuredly include the rural areas of the country. We know every village and town, even every city – no matter how large – is built on the core unit that God created in Eden – a family.

Let us take the time now to tell you just how this community with two pretty good-sized hills became Blue Mountain. Long before either a town or college was established, the Lord was not only fostering plans in General Lowrey's mind, but going before him as well, making a path. There is a wonderful story about how this old homestead became a college and a community.

When the Civil War ended, the Lowrey family was living on a small farm in North Mississippi, one mile south of the Brougher Place – also called Prospect Hill. General Lowrey, known by Civil War historians as the "Fighting Parson of Tennessee" was serving churches in North Mississippi. Also being named state evangelist, he was helping reorganize the congregations all over the state shattered by the four-year civil strife and its resulting devastation. He was called to serve as editor of *The Baptist* – a periodical that served Mississippi and Tennessee.

A friend of the family, Randolph Gipson, lived in Rienzi, Mississippi, a farming community 37 miles northeast of the Lowrey farm and 20 miles south of Corinth. Gipson came to visit the Lowreys in their somewhat isolated location. "I have made up my mind to move from Rienzi, Elder Lowrey. While I am down this way, I would like to look around to see if I can find a place to suit me. I want to be near you, so my girls can associate with your girls."

Lowrey replied: "I think the Brougher Place, which joins my land on the west, would suit you and I believe it can be bought."

The following morning Lowrey and Gipson rode over the place which amounted to a full section of land – 640 acres. This resulted in Mr. Gipson's buying the place. Returning to the farm for the night, he mentioned a problem at the supper table that evening. "General, I am rather sorry I bought that place today; the land is old and worn, much of it hilly. Though quite picturesque, it is not good farming land. Now on your place here you have good bottom land; but, Sir, you are no farmer."

From that revelation a trade would ensue. Mr. Gipson would exchange the Brougher Place for the Lowrey farm the day after he bought it. The year was 1869. Mother Berry would often say: "I'm not sure my father was fully convinced of starting a school himself when he acquired the Brougher Place. But I am convinced that God was preparing and leading M.P. Lowrey and his family to the founding and building up of Blue Mountain College and the community around it. My father was a preacher, a writer, and an editor of no small accomplishment; but up to that time, he was not a teacher. However, he had been given daughters who were being trained for that work, and a family that would give their lives in the execution of this vision."[1]

Dr. J.B. Gambrell, another distinguished Confederate officer and Baptist preacher, had long shared Lowrey's strong desire to see a Baptist school for girls established in North Mississippi and would be used of the Lord to finally convince the General that he was the man.[2] In the summer of 1872 Gambrell was assisting Elder Lowrey in a protracted meeting at Academy Baptist Church, the church Lowrey was pastoring southeast of Ripley. The week-long meeting afforded the two men of God much time for private conversation, each thinking the other was to undertake the challenging work of building a school. At some point Dr. Gambrell stated emphatically, "But, General, you have the location – a large country home suitable not only for your family, but for boarders as well; your oldest daughters are prepared to assist you; at the foot of the hill, you have an abundance of pure spring water supplying some 100 gallons of water per minute – a very real necessity in this rural setting. You have secured a post office, Sir, and you have brought a good merchant to the community. You have persuaded a fine physician, Dr. J.F. Merritt, to bring his practice among the people as well. I tell you, you are the man God has sent to build this school, my friend."[3] After days of deep discussion and prayer, Lowrey agreed to take up the gauntlet.

Just what did M.P. Lowrey rename his "Prospect Hill" once he was confirmed in his task of building a school and a community on that old farm? That is another fine story. While having somewhat settled on "Brougher Springs" as the name, an incident occurred that brought about the lyrical name the College and the town would both bear. A special guest in the Lowrey home one evening, Mrs. Annie Davidson White of Texas, formerly of North Mississippi, in sharing her love for her native home, spoke of a drive frequently made from her family home in Ripley. "General Lowrey, when I was a girl, we young people were accustomed to drive out in the buggy frequently to see the daughters of Colonel Frederick and Mrs. Carrie Brougher. Three miles this side of Ripley, there is a turn in the road where this big hill right here first looms into view. Covered with pines and cedars, in the early morning hours there is a veritable blue veil that cloaks this whole area. We girls called it 'Blue Mountain.'"

Instantly General Lowrey spoke up: "That's it! That's my name – Blue Mountain!"[4]

Well, we shall talk more about the history of Blue Mountain College and the families who made it the special place it is. As a matter of fact, later I want you to meet a very good friend of mine – Anna Jackson Quinn. She is a Blue Mountain Girl, a true and dear friend of my sweet old home, and an accomplished teacher, historian, and writer. Yes, Anna's love for literature would make her one of the first to remind you that Blue Mountain was the hometown which Tennessee Williams chose for his character Amanda Wingfield in his play *The Glass Menagerie*. I shall always wonder just who Amanda Wingfield was among our childhood friends!

All right, now that you know how we began, come with me, out our front gate here in the white picket fence. Let us take a walk in the village of Blue Mountain, a small town in the north Mississippi hills, nestled on just a little over one square mile of land – two reasonably high knolls with a lovely valley running between. Our first stop will be right across Main Street to that lovely shady spot you see with the garden bench. This, my dear, is the spot where the Blue Mountain train depot stood. It pains me to say this is where the depot *was*. It was such a delightful center of both arrivals and departures. From our front porch we saw so many of these comings and goings – comings with expectations and goings with sad farewells.

The Blue Mountain Train Depot, circa 1950

In his wisdom, General Lowrey worked diligently to build up this small community around the area of the college he would soon establish. He realized transportation was an essential element. He persuaded Colonel William

C. Falkner, entrepreneur and great-grandfather of the author William Faulkner, to help him meet this need. The General had help in this campaign from another friend: Captain Joseph Judson "J.J." Guyton, (1840-1919), father of our dear neighbor and friend whom you have already met, Dr. David E. Guyton.

David Guyton spoke of his greatest disappointment in dealing with the personal cross he bore – blindness. "My boyhood ambition was to be a locomotive engineer. When I lost my sight in childhood, nothing about blindness hurt me so much as the fact that I could never run a train. This ardent ambition will linger with me 'til the end, with a hope that I may yet have an engine to run somewhere in the great beyond," he wrote.[5]

Dr. David E. Guyton, circa 1920

Captain J.J. Guyton owned a large farm and farm supply store at Guyton, Mississippi, which was two miles south of Blue Mountain, near where General Lowrey had lived prior to buying the Brougher place. Guyton's farm was later sold to Paul J. Rainey. Colonel Falkner had completed the railway line he built from Ripley to Middleton, Tennessee, with plans for an extension to Pontotoc, Mississippi. These are the plans that General Lowrey and Captain Guyton worked conscientiously to influence.

Falkner's train was called the Doodlebug Line; Captain Guyton was its manager. The Doodlebug in its first leg, ran from Ripley north to Middleton, and made only three roundtrips a week. The Doodlebug Line was a narrow-gauge railway, having 3'6" between rails as opposed to the standard 4'8.5". This totally limited the accessibility of the tiny locomotives, coaches, freight, and flat cars to standard tracks; and conversely, standard train engines and cars could not use the narrow rails, nor the bridge crossings which were too slim and too light to accommodate them. Therefore, transfers of shipments and people had to be made at strategic points. The Doodlebug Line had two engines: *Dolly*, a lighter, passenger-type engine and *Tanglefoot*, a somewhat heavier engine for freight. *The Tanglefoot* had three driving wheels on each side, hence its name. Later as business and demands grew, two second-hand locomotives were added. They were named *The Colonel W.C. Falkner* and *The General M.P. Lowrey*.

David Guyton shared a vivid memory regarding the construction of the track roadbed for the Doodlebug. A group of convicts from the State of Mississippi prison were being used on the track construction. One of them tried to escape and was shot. The man was brought to Blue Mountain where Mother Berry took him into her home, nursed his wound and brought him through typhoid fever. He eventually died and is buried in Blue Mountain Cemetery.[6]

Falkner did indeed run the Doodlebug Rail Line that General Lowrey needed through the sparsely populated, yet to be incorporated community of Blue Mountain in 1871[7] and, through the even smaller community of Guyton, which no longer exists. The rail line was eventually upgraded to standard gauge and brought economical rail service from Middleton, Tennessee, to Houston, Mississippi. There were many name changes. The Ripley Railroad (Doodlebug line) began using the name Ship Island, Ripley, and Kentucky in 1878, and Ship Island, Ripley, and Kentucky became Gulf and Chicago in 1890. There were numerous mergers. In 1903 Mobile, Jackson, and Kansas City bought Gulf and Chicago, which eventually became part of Gulf, Mobile and Ohio – GM&O – in the 1940s. The history of the railroad that ran through this quaint village is fascinating, but quite challenging to comprehend. Why, there were even sales of portions of Colonel Falkner's railroad line in foreclosure.[8] I must wonder what business dealings between Colonel Falkner and Mr. R.J. Thurmond led to their public dispute that left Colonel Falkner mortally shot on the streets of Ripley in November 1889. Those details are likely told in other stories.

As you can see, there is no longer a train stopping here in Blue Mountain, and consequently, no depot. The only railroad service through Blue Mountain now is a freight train that goes only as far north as Ripley. To the south the railroad right-of-way that once connected New Albany and Houston is now the Tanglefoot Trail, a lovely, paved biking trail of about 43 miles. The lonely little Blue Mountain depot was torn down in

1974 after many years of faithful service to this community. It is ironic really. In 1974, I too experienced a downturn that changed my station as well.

But in its day, what stories that depot could tell! Would you believe that at one time a men's Sunday School class met here? Yes! Indeed, it did! This is a wonderful story. A contemporary of mine, Samuel L. Godwin, born right here in Blue Mountain, was quite an enterprising fellow. Some of his many activities included a logging business, cotton dealer, café owner and even semi-professional baseball pitcher. Well, as a young man, he realized that few of his teenage friends attended Lowrey Memorial Baptist Church. He organized and taught a Sunday school class for his friends that did not meet at the church house. This class remained active for many years, growing to the point of meeting in the theatre. Later, being taught by David E. Guyton, son of a great influencer in the placement of this railroad, that class would be held in the train depot. The group included several rural gentlemen, farmers who were somewhat reluctant to attend services at Lowrey Memorial Baptist because all they had to wear was their overalls – albeit their best pair on Sunday. The Lord used two men and an old public train station to fill the need for young men, as well as older ones, to grow in their faith through the teaching of His word. Like Paul, these men, Sam Godwin and David Guyton, became "all things to all men ... for the sake of the gospel" (1Corinthians 9:22-23 The Bible, Revised Standard Version). How blessed was our community!

"Can you tell me about *The Rebel?*" you ask. Oh yes, *The Rebel,* and many trains before her brought a myriad of young ladies to this whistle stop and Blue Mountain College to begin an adventure that would impact their lives forever. One of my favorite stories about trains and their relationship to the College is the one told by the mother of the Griffin Sisters of Pontotoc, Mississippi. Six sisters came to Blue Mountain in their due time to receive the good, solid, Christian education their parents were diligently working to supply them. They all rode *The Rebel* to this hallowed destination. *The Rebel* was a special passenger train that ran for the Gulf, Mobile and Northern Railroad (and later GM&O) between 1935 and 1954. It was a sleek, lightweight diesel-electric train – very high-profile gliding through the rural countryside of Tennessee, Louisiana, Mississippi, Alabama, and Missouri. Although the train was "modern" by certain standards, its trainmen were native to the areas they served and created a "community" of sorts on rails. So familiar were the brakeman, conductors, and engineers of the railroad lines that they knew folks at every stop and became "neighbors," as it were, with the populations they served on their runs. You will recall my previous stories involving the trainmen with whom our family was acquainted. Well, it seems that there was one conductor on *The Rebel* turnaround between Houston and Middleton who was just that kind of neighbor to the Griffin Sisters of Pontotoc. Their mother loved to say that, when she boarded her third daughter on the train going north to Blue Mountain College, the conductor took the young lady's bag and said: "Well, here's another Griffin Sister headed to Jericho!"

Mrs. Griffin would always laugh and say: "I'm sure he didn't recognize Marlene, but rather the dress she was wearing as it was a 'Sunday best' handed down for the third time from her two older sisters."[9]

The Rebel, circa 1950

I recall another particularly sweet story of a young lady from Japan who had come to Blue Mountain College all the way from her homeland on a very restricted budget. By boat she came to San Francisco, then by train across country to St. Louis, where she took a train heading south. With the many connections she had to make, traveling day and night sitting in a seat, the stress of the trip made her weary. Leaving the metropolitan areas with their streetlights as numerous as the stars, she grew fearful as the train passed in the night's darkness through long stretches of open land, with no lights, no houses visible, and no landmarks to note. Extremely tired, fatigue overtook fear and she drifted to sleep.

She was awakened gently by a friendly conductor who informed her that she had reached her destination. Looking out the window, she again felt some alarm as it was the middle of the night, no one else was leaving the train, and no signs pointed the way to the College. She saw only a small plaza of dark buildings. Staying close at her side, the conductor helped her with her single suitcase and aided her as she stepped off the train. There he introduced her to a smiling night watchman with his lantern. The watchman shook hands with the conductor, thanked him for the safe arrival of this young student, and took her bag as the conductor bade her adieu and wished her good luck at college. Using his lamp light, the College night watchman guided the young lady up the hill to the campus and securely to her dorm. There the dorm mother led her to a nice clean room and soft bed in which to find rest.[10]

I have always loved trains and the bits of varied culture they seem to help scatter around the country as they wind their way through valleys and mountains, cities and hamlets. Some years ago, back in the 1960s I think, a popular singer wrote a novelty song about a hobo's life. The hobo, of course, was poor – "a man of means by no means"[11] – free or forced by circumstances to travel by hopping on a train. Hobos experienced many adventures, most of which were dangerous, lonely, and always in the shadow of utter destitution. I am not sure when hobos became prevalent in America, perhaps even as early as there were trains. Likely many soldiers following the Civil War in the 1860s, finding themselves far from home and penniless, clambered into freight trains to make their way back to their families. Then, as the American frontier opened with more expansion of the railroads, adventurers and others in search of work stealthily caught the westbound freights. And then, of course, the Great Depression of the 1930s saw an increase in the number of hobos – men with no work and no home –who would "ride the rails," as the expression went, to find a way to survive.

Living close to the track, although it happened infrequently, we did occasionally have a shabby soul approach us about a meal – most were very eager to work for the food. They usually carried a bindle, a bundle made of a cloth scrap or large bandana with corners drawn together and tied over a stick, riding on their shoulder. This was the luggage of a hobo. Once while the boys were repainting the fence, we noticed a small sketch on the outside top rail of the fence. It looked like a cat drawn with a piece of coal.

 We learned later that this was a hobo symbol. We believed it was left on our fence by some fellow who had passed our way riding the rails. It was a code to other hobos that meant a kind family lives here. Mama and I talked about what a peculiar honor that was and thought that, sometime, perhaps we had been blessed to serve in a very small way "the least of these" (Matthew 25:40c The Bible, King James Version).

You can tell I am quite the romantic about the train and its folklore in our culture. But I have prattled on long enough. I wanted you to see the whole town, but alas, so much of it, like the depot, is gone. If I close my eyes, I can see more that sat on this spot. The plaza here on this elevated west side of the track began with the beautiful First National Bank building. Of course, it wasn't always this lovely, polished concrete structure. While it has always been on this corner, at one time it was a simple white clapboard building. Then south from the bank, there were business offices, one belonging to Miss Callie D. Guyton, the sister of David E. Guyton; and one occupied by Mr. Joe Hardin Guyton, Callie and David's nephew. Another establishment in that plaza was the pressing shop (you would say dry cleaners) of Mr. T.A. Bennett and his wife, Frances Grady Bennett. They kept us all looking our best in business and formal wear. Further south was J.P. Godwin's sawmill – crossties for the railroad were milled there. My mind's eye crosses Railroad Avenue to the east side of the tracks. There I see my father's store – C.F. Palmer General Store and D.M. Palmer Fine Furniture. I see Spencer Gibbs' store, later it was Miss Gibbs' Café, and there is Blue Mountain Hardware Company. I see City Drug where everyone loved to go to buy licorice, and Mr. U.B. Holt, undertaker, where no one wanted to go. Oh, and there is Gurney & Company and Miss Nannie Merritt's millenary and B.L. Simmons' Meat Market and Mr. Winborn's blacksmith shop. I can see all the way to *The Pine Tree* where Mrs. Frances Tyler lived as a widow.

If the leaves were gone, from here I could even see Mississippi Heights Academy, the preparatory school for boys which operated from 1904 to 1957. The campus sat on the top of the east and taller of the hills that flank the Town of Blue Mountain.[12] Professor J.E. Brown (1866-1947), the superintendent, was a friend of my father. Many couples sprang from those two "fountains of youth" known as Mississippi Heights and Blue Mountain College, I can tell you.

Mississippi Heights Academy, circa 1910

Now, opening my eyes I see just the person I need for this very moment! Look who is coming out of the refreshment shop, Topper Nutrition (once the First National Bank building) – it's my friend Anna Quinn that I told you about earlier.

Anna, you are just in time to take us up the hill to Blue Mountain College. I want you to tell our friend about the College you and I both love so well and the people who made her so special.

May Queen and pages in 1939

Come, let's walk up the hill together. On campus, we'll walk by the very spot two exceptional little girls walked with the 1939 May Queen! They were my sweet six-year old Alice and her life-long dear friend Elizabeth Buchanan – youngest daughter of Mr. and Mrs. James E. Buchanan, known as Mr. Buck and Miss May Hall. *See Editor's Note at end of chapter notes for more about May Day.*

But now, as we cross under the gate to the campus, we shall "Enter to Grow in Wisdom" as so many have done before us. For you and me, Anna, it will be for yet another time; for our new friend here today, maybe it will be the first of many visits to The Hill.

College gate dedicated in 1930

Endnotes

[1] Lea S. Bennett, "Come, Children, Come," Historical Narrative Presentation – Blue Mountain College Founders Day, 2010, used with permission. Information gleaned from "Reminiscences," Modena Lowrey Berry's private papers, n.d., n.p.

[2] Sumrall, *A Light on a Hill: A History of Blue Mountain College*, 18.

[3] Bennett, "Come, Children, Come," 7 - 8.

[4] Sumrall, 18 - 19.

[5] David E. Guyton, "My Daddy and the Doodlebug," *Southern Sentinel*, March 4, 1954.

[6] Ibid.

[7] The town was incorporated in January of 1877. "History, Character, and Purpose," Catalogue of Mississippi Heights Academy, Blue Mountain, Mississippi (Session 1929 – 1930), 8.

[8] Mississippi railroad history, operation and abandonments. *https://en.wikipedia.org/wiki/Ripley_and_New_Albany_Railroad*

[9] Griffin Family Story as shared by Mary Ellen Henry Russell, Griffin granddaughter, Pontotoc Mississippi.

[10] Famiko Gabriel, "My Trip from Japan to Blue Mountain," personal story shared with Lea Bennett, June 2011.

[11] Roger Miller. Lyric from "King of the Road." Smash Records, November 1964.

[12] History of Blue Mountain and Mississippi Heights Academy. *https://hillcountryhistory.org/2016/07/10/lost-history-mississippi-heights-academy-1904/*

Editor's Note on May Day:
As the name implies, **May Day** at Blue Mountain College was a May festival (originally of old European origins) which began on campus in the early 1880s. The coming of spring and the joyous anticipation of graduation and new beginnings inspired an elaborate celebration

eventually led by the three young women's literary and service societies of the campus – Eunomians, founded in 1879; Euzelians, founded in 1882; and Modenians, founded in 1907. Original plays, ornate pageants with beautiful costuming, and the selection of a May Queen and her Court – young ladies representing the societies and class years – were all part of the festivities. Also included was a May Pole dance on the lawn with young ladies and children, dressed in their spring finery, often donning woven floral garlands and crowns. Essays, poems, historic reenactments, as well as prophecies were written, directed, and performed by students, professors, and other members of the campus family, including alumni. This was a highly entertaining endeavor with many off-campus guests, often lasting throughout a long weekend.

Through the years the celebration grew shorter and less elaborate and eventually became known as *Spring Festival* in the early 1970s. It would give way to a simpler annual event, the presentation of **Miss BMC** and the doll which she added to the historic doll collection at Guyton Library. Even later **Mr. & Miss BMC**, chosen by the student body, were presented along with their gowned and tuxedo-clad court during a morning chapel service or before an athletic event.

CHAPTER 5

FORGOTTEN THEMSELVES INTO IMMORTALITY

An excellent wife, who can find her? She is far more precious
than jewels. The heart of her husband trusts in
her, and he will have no lack of gain.
Proverbs 31:10-11
The Bible, English Standard Version

Hello, Miss Lottie, I see you have brought a friend to join us for our walk up the hill, where sits beautiful Blue Mountain College. I'm Anna Quinn.

Administration Building, circa 1916

Glad to have you, and really glad to tell you about my beloved alma mater. I know you have heard stories of our founder, General Mark Perrin Lowrey and his courageous family who all joined him in his calling to establish this school. Perhaps you know about his sons who followed him as presidents, William Tyndale (W.T.) Lowrey and Bill Green (B.G.) Lowrey; and about his great grandson, Lawrence Tyndale Lowrey. When the Lowrey "dynasty" ended in 1960, it was long-time faculty member and department chair, Wilfred C. Tyler who took the helm. Then E. Harold Fisher would occupy the President's office for many years. I'm sure you know that for over one hundred years Blue Mountain College was a school for women (although there were some outstanding male graduates during those years). With that history in mind, I am going to share our story about the College's leadership primarily from the perspective of the First Ladies. For in every case, we find the Lord using not just one, but two together, both doing their part – persevering in purpose to guide the success of Blue Mountain College.

Administration Building in 2022

SARAH HOLMES LOWREY

Sarah Holmes Lowrey
circa 1890

Sarah Holmes Lowrey, the wife of the College founder and first president, General M.P. Lowrey, was called the "real general of the family"[1] by Frances Tyler in her work, "Wives of the Presidents: Blue Mountain College, 1873-1925." Tyler, a remarkable First Lady herself, will be our focus when we enter the early 1960s era in this chapter. Her work and my own personal acquaintance with some of these women will help you realize that this women's college, now co-educational, could not have survived without the wonderful women who invested their lives here, particularly the ladies married to the presidents of the College.

For many years Sarah Holmes Lowrey took care of her large family that seemed always to include many in addition to her eleven children. She was the glue that held them together as her husband ministered to people in the area as a circuit-riding preacher, as he served his

General M.P. Lowrey
circa 1885

country in war time, as he worked to help rebuild Baptist congregations in the South after the war, and as he started the College, along with their two eldest daughters, Modena and Maggie. There was no clearer indication of her strength than the sudden, shocking death of her husband in 1885. While purchasing tickets at the train station in Middleton for the group of two faculty members and ten college students who were headed to the Cotton Exposition in New Orleans, he collapsed and died of a heart attack on February 27, 1885.[2] Though not spoken aloud, the question was on many minds: Could the College survive his loss?

When W.T. Lowrey, the eldest son in the founding family, became the president in his father's stead, and later when his brother B.G. Lowrey followed him, they often told their wives, "I need to go up and talk this over with Mother," meaning Sarah Holmes Lowrey. As she had helped General Lowrey, she continued to help her sons until her death at 71 in 1898, after enduring a broken hip the last six years of her life. Of course, in those days without the wonderful procedures like hip replacements so common today, she suffered immensely. She, also, served as an example to her two daughters-in-law, Theodosia Searcy Lowrey, wife of W.T. Lowrey, College President (1885-1898) and (1911-1925); and to Marylee Booth Lowrey, wife of B.G. Lowrey, College President (1898-1911). These women were perfect choices for the young presidents, although the girls were young when they came into the family.[3]

THEODOSIA SEARCY LOWREY

Theodosia Searcy Lowrey
circa 1925

Theodosia Searcy was in her first year at Blue Mountain College when General Lowrey died. Eldest son W.T. was at Southern Baptist Theological Seminary in Louisville, Kentucky, and fortunately had just completed his Master of Theology degree. He came home to take the reins of the College at age 27 and soon renewed his acquaintance with the lovely freshman Theodosia. Their fathers, M.P. Lowrey and J.B. Searcy of Warren, Arkansas, were colleagues in Baptist ministry, serving their respective states as co-editors of the newspaper, *The Baptist*. They were also both veterans of the Confederacy. The men and their families were long-time friends. A fondness between W.T. and Theodosia grew into genuine love during her sophomore year, and they were married when she was just seventeen. Yes, I did say she was young, didn't I?

Marriage did not blur her dream of getting a college degree. Like many young married women today, she persevered in her studies and finished her degree at Blue Mountain. After that, she went to Holbrook Normal College in Ohio for an advanced degree and returned to the College to teach mathematics. She also taught social education and Mother Craft and kept study hall. She was quite a strict disciplinarian for both the college students and the children in her own family.[4]

The College girls loved her because receptions and teas were her specialty. She kept social life interesting at the College, sponsoring receptions each Saturday when girls from the College could socialize with boys from the Mississippi Heights Academy across town, east of the

College. Miss Lottie and I agree that with a little research we might be delighted to learn that many matches for the girls were made through this socialization.

Theodosia was devoted to her children, who started arriving in 1890 with Lynn, her oldest daughter, a child that was ill most of her life.

W. T and Theodosia Lowrey circa 1886

Theodosia was diligent in taking her to doctors and taking care of her during hospital stays, even though her other children – Ruby, William Tyndale, Jr., Sara, and Searcy – all arrived by 1901. As long as they lived here in Blue Mountain, she had the help of her many Lowrey relatives on the hill. In addition to caring for her children's physical needs, she took their spiritual training very seriously, always teaching her children the Bible and having them memorize verses. After all, she had been reared in a Baptist preacher's home in Arkansas before coming to the College. The high esteem in which her children held her is evident in daughter Sara's book about her mother called *Theodosia: Gift of God.* [5]

MARYLEE BOOTH LOWREY

Marylee Booth Lowrey
circa 1910

Another daughter-in-law of Sarah Holmes Lowrey, who loved and appreciated her, was Marylee Booth Lowrey, also the daughter of a Baptist minister. Her father was the one who had married M.P. Lowrey and his bride in 1849, Reverend Abijah Howard Booth of Winona, Mississippi. Marylee came by train to Blue Mountain, as did most girls in the days before cars became prevalent. She and seven other Blue Mountain College girls were met in Ripley and carried by wagon to the College on a very rainy night on a very muddy road. She was quite impressed by the driver, B.G. Lowrey, whom she described as the "nicest looking young man that she had ever seen."[6]

Like Theodosia, her contemporary, Marylee was a student at the College at the sudden death of General Lowrey. Marylee observed the dedicated Lowrey family as they dealt with the General's death and as his son W.T. Lowrey was named his successor.

Following her graduation from Blue Mountain College, Marylee taught school in Pittsboro, Mississippi, where B.G. Lowrey was principal. From Pittsboro, she went to Holbrook Normal School in Lebanon, Ohio, as had Theodosia before her. She wanted to prepare herself more thoroughly for teaching. She returned to Blue Mountain College to teach in 1888.

B.G. had been to Tulane University in New Orleans during Marylee's sojourn in Ohio. She loved him as he did her, but Marylee did not accept his proposal of marriage. He did not have a church affiliation, and Marylee felt very strongly that she should not marry an unbeliever, a truth from Scripture she had been taught by her parents. B.G. remedied that shortfall rather soon after she had rejected his proposal at Christmas. In the spring he surrendered his life to God and joined the First Baptist Church of New Orleans. He came home in 1889 to teach. The two young sweethearts planned their wedding for July 25, 1889.[7]

B.G. taught at the College during the next nine years from 1889-1898. Marylee, from 1890 -1909, gave birth to their nine children. They lived on the campus in the B.G. House, a dormitory. B.G. became president when his older brother was called to the presidency at Mississippi College in 1898, where W.T. remained until 1911. Marylee performed her duties as wife, mother, teacher, friend, and First Lady. Her husband was in great demand as a public speaker and, as a fundraiser for the College and other good causes.

With money that Marylee received when she sold the Booth farm she had inherited, they built a bungalow for their family on the east side of

B.G. Lowrey family home in Blue Mountain

Blue Mountain and moved off the campus. Their son, Leon, had a lung condition, and the new home had a screened-in porch in back where he could sleep and breathe the fresh air. Later, B.G. and Marylee moved to Amarillo, Texas, a drier climate, to help their son. There, B.G. founded and served as president of the Amarillo Military Academy.

In 1911, W.T. and Theodosia returned to the College, realizing they were needed more here. Later, B.G. and Marylee returned to the College to help in 1919. By this time, the Mississippi State Baptist Convention had taken over the affairs of the College because of financial pressures on the proprietors – B.G. Lowrey, W.T. Lowrey, T.C. Lowrey, W.E.

Berry, and Modena Lowrey Berry.[8] B.G. looked after affairs on campus as his brother W.T. traveled for the institution.

B.G. was well known for his interest in parachurch causes related to the Baptist denomination. As a Christian lay speaker, he was part of the leadership that spoke among congregations and public assemblies in the South promoting the building of Baptist hospitals in the region. He was a member of the Southern Baptist Hospital Association. He was instrumental in the building of a Baptist Hospital in Jackson, Mississippi, as well as Memphis, Tennessee. B.G. served on the board of trustees for the Memphis Baptist Hospital for a number of years.

B.G. entered politics in 1921, ending the direct association of B.G. and Marylee with the College. He served in the U.S. House of Representatives from the Mississippi Second District until 1929.[9]

ELIZABETH VEEVE COCKROFT LOWREY

Veeve Cockroft Lowrey
circa 1950

Elizabeth Veeve Cockroft Lowrey, the first wife of Dr. Lawrence T. Lowrey, fourth president of the College and the last of the Lowreys to hold the post, became his wife in 1919 before they came to Blue Mountain in 1925. She was a great asset to him until her death in 1950. Dr. Lowrey was beloved by all of us in the college community and in the state and nation. He had many offers to leave Blue Mountain for better-paying, more prestigious institutions, but he remained President of the College from 1925 to 1960.

Veeve was born in September 1887 at Newborn, Tennessee, to State Attorney General and Mrs. S.L. Cockroft. She went to grammar school in Dyersburg, Tennessee, and graduated from high school in Memphis. She earned her B.A. degree from Blue Mountain College in 1909. After doing some graduate study, she taught in the Speech Department at the Mississippi Woman's College (later William Carey University) in Hattiesburg. She also taught at Blue Mountain College for three sessions from 1909 to 1915.[10]

The Lawrence T. Lowreys faced struggles concerning housing in Blue Mountain. Lawrence and his beloved Veeve had two children, a son Robert Booth Lowrey and a daughter Jean Lowrey, who later married Lauris M. Eek, and was consistently called Jean Lowrey Eek. The family moved into Anderson House in 1925 when he was elected President. In 1928, a fire that swept across much of Blue Mountain burned several College structures, including their home.[11] The Lowreys lost most of their furnishings and belongings. For the next ten years, they moved 11 times – to apartments in various dormitories or to a nearby house, one after another. But daughter Jean said that wherever they lived her mother "made a happy home."[12]

Veeve and Mrs. Emma Fair Armstrong, a graduate and member of the Board of Trustees, led a movement to raise money for the first President's home at Blue Mountain College. She gave the largest contribution to the beautiful colonial revival home that became a prominent new landmark on the campus. Emma expressed a desire for this building to be named "Armstrong" in honor of her deceased husband, John K. Armstrong. He had inspired and challenged her to initiate the fund that would build the home.[13]

Armstrong, Home of the President since 1939

Living a life of devoted servanthood, Veeve Cockroft Lowrey spent many of the last years of her life taking care of her aging relatives or those of her husband. According to Mrs. Elma Lois McKinstry, English professor at the College and longtime friend and traveling companion of Mrs. Lowrey, Veeve Lowrey was wise, tactful, full of sympathetic understanding of others, and a loyal friend. She pointed out "her unmeasured devotion" to Blue Mountain College. They served together in the Mississippi Congress of Parents and Teachers, Mrs. Lowrey as state president and Mrs. McKinstry as state publicity chairman. Mrs. McKinstry praised Veeve's intellectual and leadership ability and "her delightful sense of humor that sweetened and saved many a situation."[14]

In his memorial tribute, published under the title "She Forgot Herself into Immortality," in January 1951, Dr. David E. Guyton said:

> In the death of Mrs. Lowrey, this neighborhood has lost one of its loveliest and most useful women. Modest in every relationship of life, and yet an unfailing tower of strength and a gracious inspiration to those whose lives touched her own, she has left an influence for good, for lofty everyday living, and for God and the Kingdom of Christ here on earth that will continue to bless innumerable men and women made better because she passed their way. Mrs. Veeve Cockroft Lowrey will remain a perpetual benediction as long as goodness and grace lend meaning and majesty to life.[15]

ERNESTINE H. EASTLAND LOWREY

***Ernestine E. Lowrey
circa 1960***

Ernestine H. Eastland Lowrey, the second wife of President Lawrence T. Lowrey, came to Blue Mountain College in March 1952. He had known her well for many years because her deceased husband was his first cousin. She was born in Alabama, but she had lived most of her life in Baton Rouge, Louisiana, where she continued as a director of Southern National Life Insurance Company and as president of the Eastland Foundation even after her marriage to Dr. Lowrey. A graduate of Louisiana State University, she was gifted in both piano and art.

Upon coming to the College, her special project was the renovation and decoration of the President's home. Mrs. Lowrey (called Tina by her friends) said: "This lovely house was a delight and challenge to do from the ground floor up to the attic."[16] Following the renovation, the Lowreys entertained many guests in Armstrong, such as other college presidents, leaders of the Baptist world, politicians, poets, writers, and musicians. In addition, she loved to landscape at Armstrong and on campus, planting flower beds and rose gardens.

Mrs. Lowrey travelled with her husband to places like Burma, Cambodia, Vietnam, India, and Thailand. During their travels they often visited in the homes of foreign students going to Blue Mountain. With costumes and pictures from her travels, she gave talks to the students about these faraway places.[17]

Although continuing interests in Baton Rouge took her away part of each month, Ernestine Lowrey made a lasting impact at Blue Mountain College during the eight years she lived here before Dr. Lowrey's retirement. She also established scholarships that continue to be given today.

MARY FRANCES LANDRUM TYLER

Frances Landrum Tyler
circa 1965

One of the finest examples of womanhood to those privileged to know her, Frances Landrum Tyler was the First Lady of Blue Mountain College for only five years, from 1960-1965. President Wilfred C. Tyler assumed leadership of the College when Dr. Lawrence T. Lowrey retired in 1960, but Dr. Tyler died unexpectedly in 1965.

Dr. David E. Guyton, in writing about Mother Berry, stated that "A good woman is the noblest work of God."[18] I just missed knowing Mother Berry as she died in 1942, but I did know and love Wilfred C. and Frances Tyler, along with their wonderful children – Landrum and Carol, who were my contemporaries at Blue Mountain College in the early sixties. I first met Mrs. Tyler when she spoke at a graduation ceremony at my community's high school. One of my relatives was graduating, so I attended the exercises with my parents. Even as a small child I was totally impressed with her spritely air and her lovely demeanor. From that evening I determined I must go to Blue Mountain College. How many more alumnae must be out there who came because of Frances Tyler! When I arrived on campus in 1958, the Tylers were there in teaching positions as Dr. Lawrence T. Lowrey was in his last years as president.

Frances Tyler was born in Laurel, Mississippi, in 1906, to Mr. and Mrs. G. B. Landrum. She was destined to be a musician as her father bought her a piano when she was only two weeks old. Although her father passed away when she was four, music was a way she shared herself all of her life. For example, at my invitation she came to my home church to lead the music time with the children when I directed Vacation Bible School. She was in great demand as a speaker at churches throughout Mississippi and beyond. Anyone fortunate enough to visit in her home remembers that, no matter what season of the year, she would play "Joy to the World" on her pink piano in the parlor and for loftier occasions on the baby grand piano in the living room. She always asked her guests to sing along. Another tradition was her love for candles. Never did a dinner guest enjoy her table without her candle-lighting ceremony. On her table she had a three-pronged candelabrum, given to the Tylers as a wedding present, on which Mrs. Tyler would light candles – one for the past, one for the present, and one for the future.

"Anna, may I interrupt you to tell you both a story about that candle ceremony and what it meant to one BMC College student I knew?"

"Of course, Miss Lottie."

"This young lady was newly married and lived near the College. Her husband worked in the area and, like so many young marrieds, they had only one vehicle. So, I would often see this young lady walking in Blue Mountain – to town for groceries, to the post office, to visit friends and neighbors. She frequently stopped by to see me when I would be on the porch or in the garden. We enjoyed good conversation. While attending one of Mrs. Tyler's classes, she became friends with Mrs. Tyler and soon began visiting her at her home – the Pine Tree. One afternoon, on her return trip from an informal afternoon tea at Mrs. Tyler's, this young lady, Virginia by name, stepped up on the porch to give a quick hello. I could tell she was enthralled and asked how the tea went."

"It was divine," Virginia answered. "As we were preparing to leave, she asked us to gather around for prayer. I shall always remember her sweet salute:"

> We light three candles for your life,
> Slender, tall, and fair;
> Each one a fire bloom, each one a prayer.
> The first we light for memories,
> The next for days that are.
> The last we light for days to come,
> That beckon like a star.[19]

Thank you for that story, Miss Lottie. It certainly illustrates the gracious and meaningful impact Mrs. Tyler had on the students at Blue Mountain College. Now, back to Frances' early life.

When young Frances' father died, her mother went back to school to get a teaching degree. She carried five-year-old Frances to school with her when she began teaching. As a result, Frances graduated from high school when she was 16. When Frances was seven, she and her little brother G.B. were blessed with a loving stepfather, Charles Thomas Walters. She referred to her mother's marriage as the time when "we got married." Three little sisters were born to the union.

Frances was an outstanding student. After serving as student body president at Laurel High School, she graduated as valedictorian of her class. At graduation she received "the highest honor given, the Lauren Rogers Prize, for citizenship and leadership."[20] Her daughter Carol Tyler Townsend told me that Wilfred Tyler was teaching mathematics at Laurel High School after he had completed his degree at Mississippi College while playing football. He was very impressed by his young student and sent her a dozen red roses for graduation. After her graduation, they went their separate ways – Frances, to Mississippi Woman's College in Hattiesburg (now William Carey University) and Wilfred, to Louisville Baptist Theological Seminary in Kentucky (now The Southern Baptist Theological Seminary) to major in Greek and Hebrew.

In college, Frances continued to be the outstanding young lady she was in high school. She graduated with many honors and awards, served as president of the student government, and earned her degree in music and in English. From college, she went to Louisville to pursue a ministry degree. Here she and Wilfred reconnected. He proceeded to show her all over Louisville. They ushered in the symphony. Frances was much impressed with this "erudite gentleman who liked Bach and Tchaikovsky."[21] The courtship continued as they worked on their degrees. In Wilfred, Frances always had a male escort for all the social affairs, church activities, and civic concerts. Frances graduated with a master's degree in religious education and returned to Mississippi to accept the position of Young People's Leader of the Mississippi Woman's Missionary Union (W.M.U). During the 18 months that Frances worked in Jackson, Wilfred received his doctorate from the Louisville seminary and went to Maryland as pastor of the College

Avenue Baptist Church in Annapolis. He also worked on convincing Frances to marry him. In November 1932, he wrote Frances' mother a letter:

> Dear Mrs. Walters:
> I have just come to my room from the Union Thanksgiving Service ... How full my heart is of gratitude to God and to you for all the joy and blessing which is now and will be mine because of Frances. The beauty of her life is the result of God's and your handiwork, and, of course, her own choices. But even her choices have been from the good you have, throughout her life, presented to her. I cannot express my sense of humility and appreciation for the privilege of always serving her, but I do love her and believe her to be the dearest girl in the world. What a debtor I am to you!
> Sincerely,
> Another son, Wilfred[22]

Frances and Wilfred were married December 28, 1932, at First Baptist Church of Laurel.

They served in Annapolis for about four years during which they volunteered to go to China for Christian work. Frances, however, was pregnant with her first child, and her doctor warned them not to go because of her precarious condition. They were sorely disappointed. Their baby later came stillborn, and Frances nearly died. She remained in a weakened condition for a long time. Once she recovered, sadly the opening to go to China was no longer available.

Mr. Perrin Lowrey, brother of President Lawrence T. Lowrey, was in Baltimore. He and Dr. Tyler played golf together. Carol Tyler Townsend said that the Lowreys "courted Daddy," encouraging her parents to come to Blue Mountain College. They gave up their dream of going to China and followed what they believed was God's leading to Blue Mountain where Dr. Tyler became Head of the Biblical Studies Department in 1936. Townsend said that her father loved teaching Bible, especially to women, and never wanted to become President of the College. When he became President at the urging of the Lowreys and the Board of

Trustees, his daughter Carol said that he always saw himself as not permanent but "standing in the gap."[23]

How like Abraham and Sarah they were! God told them to go and they went! Mississippi was quite a journey from Maryland in 1936. They moved into two rooms in Hearn-Jennings dormitory.

According to their daughter, they prayed for a baby and a house. Soon after, she became pregnant with their son Landrum, born in 1939. Daughter Carol came in 1942. Looking for more space, they moved to the Joe Hardin Guyton house, then to Mr. Perrin Lowrey's house, and even to other homes. Dr. Tyler finally went to President Lawrence T. Lowrey to resign, saying he must have better housing for his family. They had lived in one old house after another. Dr. Lowrey got busy and got funding for the Stewart House, the Bible professor's home. They lived in Lowrey dormitory while the house was being built. So after more than 10 years, the Tylers finally had adequate housing for their family in Blue Mountain and were here to stay.[24]

Carol loved remembering the study off the living room where her father wrote Sunday school lessons at a table specifically given to the Bible professor. She also recalled the carving on the living room shutters which said, "I am the light of the world" and "Be of good cheer for I have overcome the world." She described how their family would return from being away and kneel in front of the fireplace to thank

Frances and Wilfred Tyler, circa 1963

God for their home. Her father moved the family once more – to Armstrong, the President's home, in 1960.[25]

In a Founders Day program on November 7, 1980, honoring Mrs. Tyler, Frances and Wilfred Tyler were called "the perfect complement to each other in every way as they worked together."[26] They had co-authored columns in magazines and written books together. They had traveled all over the South as program speakers, especially during the summer months. Mrs. Tyler taught a very popular class of Old Testament in the department which her husband chaired for many years. She loved the W.M.U. and served as the recording secretary of the state organization for 19 years. In addition, she wrote for the publications of that organization where she no doubt influenced many young readers to be mission-minded.

After her dear husband died on April 7, 1965, Frances moved from Armstrong to The Pine Tree, her home on Highway 15 in Blue Mountain. As therapy, she began taking classes at the University of Mississippi and received first a master's degree then a doctorate in 1974 when she was 68. She was a dedicated lifelong learner, teacher, musician, writer, and speaker. The work of Frances and Wilfred C. Tyler represents 45 years of devotion to the College and to many people living all over the world.[27]

MARTHA HUGGINS FISHER

Martha Huggins Fisher
circa 2001

The E. Harold Fishers came as the "First Family" in 1965 and remained until 2001, making Martha Fisher the longest tenured First Lady to date. She was already very familiar with the College since she had lived as a child in nearby Oxford with her parents, Naomi and Clyde G. Huggins and her two sisters and brother. She attended University High School in Oxford. She followed her two older sisters to Blue Mountain College, where she graduated in 1952 with a degree in Business Education. President Fisher enjoyed telling the story of having courted her during her college years in the Lowrey Dormitory where the same curtains were hanging when he and his family arrived to begin his time as president.

Following graduation, Martha taught at Shaw High School in the Mississippi Delta. She said that when she and Harold were engaged, she came home to Oxford to get married when he completed graduate school. However, Uncle Sam had other plans. After basic training he was sent to Japan for eighteen months. When he returned, they were married in Oxford.[28]

When he became President of Blue Mountain College in 1965, they brought with them from Jackson, Mississippi, their three small children – Barbara, Hal, and Laura, ages 8, 4, and 3, respectively. The children grew up in Armstrong, and both daughters are graduates of Blue Mountain College and the son, of Mississippi College. The children are now married and have presented the Fishers with seven grandchildren.

Mrs. Fisher said that people would offer compliments about how nice the children were and ask how she did it. She told them, "I did it one day at a time."[29]

The Fisher family, 1965

I observed Mrs. Fisher as a gracious hostess at Armstrong and at many events held on campus, always standing by her husband's side, greeting guests warmly when they came to the campus. She would likely be wealthy if she had a dollar for every reception she hosted or event she attended when students were honored after a recital, a play, or a concert.

Some of my fondest memories are being at Armstrong as an alumna myself, helping her host receptions for seniors and their families after graduation practice each spring. Always very active in the Blue Mountain College Alumnae Association, serving as president of the local club and as vice-president and secretary of the National Alumnae Association, she had many friends who enjoyed bringing goodies for such occasions and helping her serve at Armstrong or at the Whitfield Faculty Parlor.

I was in a unique position to observe her as we were both faculty members at Blue Mountain College together for several years. She had majored in Business Education at Blue Mountain College, earned a master's degree in Business Education from the University of Mississippi, and joined the Department of Business Education at the College in 1970. She taught until her retirement in 1996 after 26 years. Also, she designed and taught a personal development course for freshman students. Many students will tell you that because of Mrs. Fisher's class in social etiquette they know how to set a table for a formal dinner and how to choose the correct eating utensil when faced with an array of them.

The 1989 *Mountaineer*, the yearbook for the College, was dedicated to her by the students for her "unselfish devotion to Blue Mountain College," for her "precision and commitment to excellence which are evident in every facet of her life – family, school, community, and church." Editor Lisa Sandlin said that Mrs. Fisher "seeks to inspire these same qualities in her students" and "provides an example worthy of emulation."[30]

Students describing Mrs. Fisher often used the words: "professional," "very business-like," "rigorous in the classroom," and "dignified." Yet there was a gentle side of Martha Fisher that proved her servant's spirit. The mother of a certain student shares a story that illustrates this well. It seems that this young lady had from early childhood intended to follow in the footsteps of her mother, grandmother, and aunts in attending Blue Mountain College. However, after an "exploring careers" field trip she took with her high school class, the young lady felt like court-reporting was the career she would pursue. Blue Mountain College did not offer courses in that area of study. Knowing the young lady's sincere desire to come to Blue Mountain (as well as the heart of her mother), Mrs. Fisher spent a considerable amount of time developing an arrangement between the BMC Business Education Department and the University of Mississippi's School of Applied Sciences: Legal Studies. In the arrangement the young lady would take Judicial Reporting Procedures classes at The University of Mississippi and receive full credit for that work toward her Bachelor of Science from Blue Mountain College. This service above and beyond the call of duty was deeply appreciated by all concerned and showed that Mrs. Fisher was a dedicated educator who cared about students.

Her leadership skills were shared through her many associations in the local community and the state. She was active in the Mississippi Federation of Women's Clubs, president of the Blue Mountain Woman's Club, president of the American Association of University Women (AAUW) local chapter, and president of Upsilon Chapter of Delta Kappa Gamma, a professional society for women educators. Through all of these associations, she promoted Blue Mountain College and its program of Christian education and her husband as its president. Throughout their tenure they were loyal members of Lowrey Memorial Baptist Church, where she served as church treasurer and taught Sunday School.

The tribute paid Martha Huggins Fisher by the Blue Mountain College National Alumnae Association in 1997 as its Alumna of the Year puts an exclamation mark to her remarkable work as First Lady:

> Characterized by strength and dignity, the First Lady of Blue Mountain College is an inspiration to all. She has raised three children, held countless leadership positions, continued her own education, educated hundreds of college students, and has gently guided an entire college toward excellence. The alumnae association is honored to recognize Martha Huggins Fisher, a graduate who exemplifies the finest attributes of a Blue Mountain College alumna.[31]

Mrs. Fisher depicts her years as First Lady by identifying with the poet Tagore saying, "My time as First Lady was duty, service and joy, and I tried to do all of that with gratitude, loyalty, grace and yes, stamina."[32] She quotes Tagore:

> I slept and dreamt that life was joy
> I awoke and saw that life was service
> I acted and beheld service was joy.[33]

Miss Lottie, these are the first ladies who served Blue Mountain College. Thank you for letting me share their stories. I know you knew them all personally. You will agree with me when I tell our new friend here that they were women who served the College faithfully alongside their outstanding husbands.

I do agree with you fully, Anna, and am glad you were able to join us on this part of our walk. Indeed, to think on the leadership couples at Blue Mountain is to be reminded of Priscilla and Aquilla, the faithful New Testament saints that God had so beautifully yoked together in service. Yes, these women worked with distinction, joy, grace, and loyalty to their calling as committed life partners in the presidencies of Blue Mountain College and its community. With dedication to the College and gratitude to God, they labored, forgetting *themselves* into immortality.

Endnotes

[1] Tyler, Frances L. "Wives of the Presidents: Blue Mountain College, 1873-1925." Unpublished research paper at the University of Mississippi, March 24, 1972. Archives, Guyton Library, Blue Mountain, Mississippi.

[2] Sumrall, Robbie Neal. *A Light on a Hill: A History of Blue Mountain College.* Nashville, Tennessee: The Benson Printing Company, 1947, 25.

[3] Tyler, Wives.

[4] Ibid.

[5] Ibid.

[6] Ibid.

[7] Ibid.

[8] Sumrall, 41-42.

[9] Biographical Directory of the United States Congress. *https://www.bioguide.congress.gov*

[10] "Blue Mountain College Continues to Grow: Cockroft Residence Hall Formally Dedicated at BMC," *Blue Mountain College Bulletin,* May 1969.

[11] "Silhouettes of Great Ladies." Unpublished Founders Day Program on November 3, 1972. Archives, Guyton Library, Blue Mountain, Mississippi.

[12] Ibid.

[13] Sumrall, 55.

[14] Silhouettes.

[15] Guyton, David E. "In Memoriam: Mrs. Lawrence T. Lowrey," *Blue Mountain College Bulletin,* January 1951.

[16] Silhouettes.

[17] Ibid.

[18] David E. Guyton, *Mother Berry of Blue Mountain* (Nashville, Tennessee: Broadman Press, 1942), 8.

[19] This was a short version of a longer poem that was a blessing for a home and family which Mrs. Tyler often quoted.

[20] "Frances Tyler: This Is Your Life." Unpublished Founders Day Program on November 7, 1980. Archives, Guyton Library, Blue Mountain, Mississippi.

[21] Carol Tyler Townsend, Interview Notes by Anna Jackson Quinn, June 8, 2018.

[22] "Frances Tyler: This Is Your Life."

[23] Townsend.

[24] Ibid.

[25] Ibid.

[26] "Frances Tyler: This Is Your Life."

[27] Ibid.

[28] Martha Huggins Fisher, Email Interview by Anna J. Quinn, August 2, 2021.

[29] Ibid.

[30] "1989 Yearbook Dedicated to Mrs. Fisher." *Blue Mountain College Bulletin,* Spring 1989.

[31] "Martha Fisher Honored as 1997 Alumna of the Year," *Blue Mountain College Bulletin,* April-June 1997.

[32] Email Interview, Quinn.

[33] From *Gitanjali* (Bengali: গীতাঞ্জলি), Tagore's best-known collection of poetry, for which he was awarded the Nobel Prize in Literature in 1913. *https://www.eatmy.news/2020/10/life-history-and-works-of-rabindranath.html*

Editor's Note: As you learned, Miss Lottie knew the First Ladies remembered in this chapter. They are, in fact, all the first ladies to date. The presidents who have followed are outstanding women whose husbands, often called "First Gentlemen" by the students, have worked alongside them: President Emerita, Bettye Rogers Coward, 2001-2012, married to Tom Coward; President Barbara Childers McMillin, 2012-present, married to Larry McMillin.

CHAPTER 6

WHERE TWO OR THREE ARE GATHERED

Not forsaking the assembling of ourselves together...
but exhorting one another
Hebrews 10:25
The Bible, King James Version

In dedicating his book *Lowrey Memorial Baptist Church: The First Hundred Years 1879-1979*, Dr. W. Carey Hearn wrote:

> This book is written to celebrate the anniversary of a church that for one hundred years has served in times of trial and in times of celebration as the "handmaiden of the Lord." It is dedicated to all present and past members and all others who have loved Lowrey Memorial Baptist Church and who have shared its mission and contributed to its heritage.[1]

Editor's note: This chapter is sincerely dedicated to "all others" – the myriad students, faculty, staff, and administrators of Blue Mountain College, sojourners in the tiny village of Blue Mountain and surrounding areas who worshiped, experienced the grace and mercies of the living God, and pledged their allegiance to His Cause. To those who were baptized; who were joined in holy wedlock; who were taught, edified, and equipped for service; who heard and rejoiced in the message of the Gospel of Jesus Christ in the hallowed refuge of the church that met as Lowrey Memorial Baptist Church.

Lowrey Memorial Baptist Church, built in 1908 in Blue Mountain,
Mississippi; named in memory of Mark Perrin Lowrey (1828-1885),
founder of Blue Mountain Female Institute,
now Blue Mountain College.
Reuben Harrison Hunt, of R.H. Hunt and Company,
architectural firm of Chattanooga, Tennessee.[2]

Oh, friend, as I stand with you here, on the front campus of Blue Mountain College, looking up at the beautiful old, white church building known as Lowrey Memorial Baptist Church, my heart is flooded with memories. I feel the joys, remember the tears, cherish the truths, uphold the precious doctrines, and so fondly recall sharing in the earthly lives of so many people my family knew there. I think of countless hours spent through the years at that church house by my family – especially by my father, Charles F. Palmer; by my husband, Lon Donnell; and by me, Lottie Palmer Donnell. For the Lord blessed us all, not only to be nurtured in our spirits, fed from His Word, and edified by the fellowship of our brothers and sisters in Christ, but also to serve Him among the throng that once met in that church house. It was our joy to labor in keeping the records as church clerks, treasurers, and in other capacities through the years. In its earliest days it was called Macedonia Baptist Church, meeting in a log structure high atop this hill on the ridge running west, long before the community was called Blue Mountain. The original churchyard cemetery remains up there and is joined by the city cemetery as well now. That original church group was organized as a mission under the auspices of the Mississippi Baptist Association, established in 1806 while Mississippi was still a territory; it served for a time, as the only Baptist church in the region.

Following the Civil War, General Mark Perrin Lowrey and his large family moved into this verdant area and encouraged other families to come to the vicinity. He began serving that Church as pastor. Then with the establishment of Blue Mountain Female Institute in 1873 and the population steadily increasing in the area of the College, the original Macedonia Church building and its location became inadequate for the growth of the congregation, which included students from the College. In 1879 the assembly built another meeting house nearer the College on property donated by M. P. Lowrey; it was dedicated on November 13,

Lowrey Memorial

1879, as Blue Mountain Baptist Church.[3] Regarding the original property and building belonging to the church called Macedonia, a committee determined that the building belonged to "the brethren west of where the church stands,"[4] on the high ridge above and west of the College campus. These brethren would eventually reconstitute their church body approximately five miles north of the first site at a lower elevation in a community known as Deentown in the area called Tippah Bottom. They retained the name Macedonia Baptist Church. It stands and meets to this day. You may recall my grandfather, Louis Pearl "L.P." Cossitt served that church as pastor at one time.

Now, as I stand here at Lowrey church, I think of so many things I want to tell you. While it is beautiful and stately, this church house is more than brick and mortar, stained glass, and a four-story tower. It is the meeting house indeed. But the church – the kingdom of God – is in the hearts and souls of the blood-bought saints *who come together* in that brick and mortar. They come together in unity and oneness of purpose: to ascribe to the Lord his "worthship" – to worship and adore Him for He is worthy. The church is the seat of the royal priesthood to which God has called us (I Peter 2:9); it is the pillar and ground of truth (I Timothy 3:15); it is the household of faith where we learn by precept and practice to do good to all people. (Galatians 6:10) For these causes and more, it is truly *the people* who fill my mind as I think on Lowrey Memorial Baptist Church. The first two of those people who come to my mind are my beloved parents.

My father, Charles F. Palmer, was born in 1862 on the homestead his family established in 1830. He attended secondary school in Blue Mountain, then completed studies at George Peabody College in Nashville, Tennessee. After teaching in Florida for two years, he returned to Tippah County to manage his family's homeplace after of the death his father, John Dederick Palmer. After marrying my mama in 1885 at Blue Mountain Baptist Church, he established his mercantile business on the east side of the railroad in Blue Mountain with a greater interest in commerce than agriculture. He also worked as the depot agent for the railroad. His church affiliation was Blue Mountain Baptist Church. In 1891 he became clerk of the church which was now called Lowrey Memorial Baptist Church. He served until 1916. Papa was also active in governance in the community. He was elected treasurer for the Town of Blue Mountain in 1902 and was a "trusted official" of the Bank of Blue Mountain.[5]

Mama, Miss Allie to so many, loved the church and its fellowship, taking great delight in providing bouquets of fresh flowers for worship services and other occasions. Her roses were considered the hallmark of her garden. She fully invested herself in the management of her home and the cares of her family and her church family. At the time of her death (1955), she was the oldest member of Lowrey Memorial Baptist Church and the one with the longest continual membership – 75 years.[6] She loved to reminisce about the "old days" in the church, about brush arbor meetings, camp meetings and about coming to the church for membership during her eighteenth year.

In the early days of our country's history, say from the 1700s to mid-1900s, communities often celebrated the Gospel message under a brush arbor. A brush arbor was a temporary structure, open-sided and made from rough vertical poles driven into the ground. The top frame was also made of long poles. Often the poles were cut from somewhere very near the site of the gathering. For the roof, brush, cut branches, boughs, or even hay would be laid over the horizontal poles on the top. These structures were not unlike the Old Testament "booths" spoken of in Leviticus. The last festival of the Jewish year was the Festival of Booths. For one week the people lived in booths or huts made of boughs, at the Lord's command:

> Now on the first day you shall take for yourselves the foliage of beautiful palm branches and boughs of leafy trees and willows of the brook... You shall live in booths for seven days...so that your generations may know that I had the sons of Israel live in booths when I brought them out from the land of Egypt: I am the Lord your God.
> Leviticus 23:40-43, The Bible, New American Standard Version

In our country these protracted Gospel meetings, later called revivals, could last for days or even weeks, with many people traveling for miles to attend the meetings. They would stay in homes as guests or even camp on the grounds. In the early years in America, these meetings were held by itinerant ministers or preachers who rode a circuit through rural communities. Much preparation was done to make ready for these gatherings, which were typically held in the early spring before planting, mid-summer after crops were laid by, and fall after harvesting was over.

These meetings were often held near a crossroads of a well-traveled area, or the proposed site of a future church house, and in later years, on the grounds of an established church, during a special celebration. Lowrey Memorial Baptist Church was no exception to this practice of hosting protracted meetings and was well known for having outstanding preachers.

Dr. J.B. Searcy, father of First Lady Theodosia Searcy Lowrey, was one of the exceptional preachers frequently holding these meetings at Lowrey Memorial. Eventually he would be called from Arkansas to the pastorate at First Baptist Church in Corinth.[7] First Baptist of Corinth was organized in the summer of 1855, when Mark Perrin Lowrey and about a dozen other believers met under an oak tree. Lowrey would serve as the first pastor at the Corinth church. In 1856 the church with 19 members was recognized by the Chickasaw Baptist Association.[8]

"Meeting Under the Oak Tree"
Painted by Les Rasberry

Mama and Papa often told stories of these meetings and other wonderful experiences they shared at Lowrey Memorial. You know Mama always smiled when she talked about coming to the church for membership in 1888. She and her good friend, Virginia Gayle McWilliams, came on the same day to ask for "a home in the church." Virginia Gayle's maternal grandfather was Peter Smith Gayle, a frontier Baptist circuit rider who was instrumental in the organization of First Baptist Church in Nashville, Tennessee, and served as its pastor in the early 1830s. He also served as pastor of First Baptist Church of Memphis, Tennessee.[9]

Virginia Gayle's father was Dr. Andrew Riley McWilliams, who was born in Maury County, Tennessee, and was educated at Botanico Medical College in Memphis. He and his wife had come in the early days of Blue Mountain Female College to enroll their two daughters. He also served as the College physician. Virginia Gayle married George Richardson Donnell, a landowner of Tunica, Mississippi, in 1883. The couple had four children: Alonzo, Hassell, George, and Norman.[10]

I'm sure you caught that first name "Alonzo," didn't you? Yes, that was my own husband. Virginia Gayle and my mother Allie were school mates who both joined Lowrey church on the same day and were later grandmothers to our four children.

Remarkable, isn't it? However, Virginia Gayle was widowed in 1890, with four small boys to bring up. In 1892 she married Dr. William M. Krauss, the first radiologist in Memphis; but she would live only five more years, dying in 1897.

Her boys were educated in boarding schools and often spent the summers in Blue Mountain with their maternal grandfather, Dr. McWilliams.[11] Yes, as I fondly recall, the first place I ever saw Alonzo McWilliams Donnell was sitting on a pew at Lowrey Church. And well, as they say, the rest is history.

My mama and my papa took seriously the admonition of Hebrews 10:25, believing that church attendance was more than just a directive from the Lord, but that like all the commands of our good God, they are given to us for our own well-being.

Young Alonzo at college. Could he be reading a letter from his friend Lottie?

My parents understood how dark and fallen our world is and how much we need the love and fellowship of like-minded Christians. I declare once again my great love for them and my gratitude for my upbringing in their care. Like them I found the church to be, not only the pillar and ground of truth, but also the body of Christ, the body of believers who support each other, bear one another's burdens, and share the sweet blessings of fellowship in the Gospel of our Lord.

I think of so many friends as I glance up at that beautiful old church house, friends like Corinne and David E. Guyton, our neighbors and colleagues. Both had servant's hearts. Corrine, originally from New Albany, was a member of the Daughters of the American Revolution and Colonial Dames. She taught history at the College for 24 years. David, blind from the age of twelve after an accident, was a professor at the College, teaching history for over 50 years. He also taught French, German, and English. His student readers will smile warmly as they recall being in this couple's lovely home, helping the Professor prepare for his classes by reading the upcoming lesson aloud. All his former students will recall his uncanny skill at learning their names and recognizing them by the sound of, not only their voices, but the cadence of their footsteps.

You know, it was common way back in my day for folks to make many, many things by hand – from tools, to linens, and clothing, to greeting cards, and gifts, and many other items that people just "run to town" and buy now. I can recall the time when girls painted their own china, working years to complete a full set for their hope chests. They tatted – and I do not mean marked up their bodies with ink – I mean the making of fine lace by working a small shuttle made of metal, or wood, or ivory. The shuttle was used to help tie tiny knots in thread at strategic points to form lace.

Ah, what I'd give to sit out on the porch with Mama and hear her shuttle whispering its busy little clicks as her dexterous fingers seemed to magically make lace. I might then take the lace to sew with carefully hidden blind-stitches on the edge of a new set of fine cotton pillowcases for one of the couples in the church who was getting married. I might use the lace on the hem of a handkerchief where I had drawn and stitched pansies in one corner for a young lady graduating. Yes, in those days people in the church and the community gathered 'round their young folks in social celebrations, bringing food to share and giving gifts – most gifts homemade and handmade and all very practical.

Now, I've let myself get carried away. I was going to tell you about the handmade greeting card that Corinne and David sent us in December 1953. In it was a poem written by this winsome couple to and about our family. They were both so gifted. The rhyme went like this:

May every Donnell of the lot,
Those out of town, those on the spot,
>   In every game of '54,
>   Achieve a gratifying score.

May Mrs. Palmer, bless her heart!
Keep well to play her royal part.
>   May Lonnie toe Miss Lottie's line
>   And never whimper, never whine.

May Dr. Mac and dear Lorrayne
Their proudest, grandest goal attain.
>   May George and all his loving clan
>   Put over every cherished plan.

May Tom and Marjorie and Charles
Escape life's little stings and snarls.
>   May every day to each of these
>   Bring just the things that always please.

May Alice find in Vanderbilt
Those values that can never wilt
>   And may she marry, not too soon,
>   A man to make each month a June.

Corinne and I are proud to claim
As friends indeed, not just in name,
>   Our Donnell neighbors tried and true,
>   May God be good to each of you.[12]

Corrine and David Guyton were indeed remarkable people. Despite his blindness, he was an incredible asset to the church and the community. For example, you may recall that he taught a Sunday School class at the train depot in Blue Mountain. I have the remnant of an old

DEPOT SUNDAY SCHOOL —This Men's Bible Class of the Blue Mountain, Miss., Baptist Church has been meeting in the G.M.&O. depot waiting room almost a quarter century. Taught by blind David Guyton, poet-professor at Mountain College. It is of the most unusual in state.

Blind Man Brings God's Word To A Hot, Gray Little Depot

By A. G. WEEMS
Staff Correspondent

BLUE MOUNTAIN, Miss., Aug. 8.—I sat in the waiting room of the G. M. & O. Depot in this Tippah County town and listened as a blind man spoke. There were 27 other men in the room, and the weather were hard, the weather uncomfortably hot.

The blind man stood by the door in his shirt sleeves, he talked he clasped and unclasped his strong hands, and his head from side to side "looking" in turn at each of those had come to listen. The big stove, which warms the "Rebel's" passengers as they wait in the Winter, sat like a huge, ugly, unwanted sore thumb in the middle of the room. The ticket window was closed.

A Sunday School Class

It was 10 o'clock in the morning and it was Sunday—and Dave Guyton was teaching his Sunday School class.

As I looked around, I saw other men without coats, many even without ties. A few were chewing tobacco. But as Dave failed all

Jackson, father-in-law of Jess Gowdy, Blue Mountain member-philosopher of whom we last year. Professor Jack taught English grammar old Mississippi Heights upon the hill across the road.

At one time the class in the local theater, but convened every Sunday for the past 20 years—we took it over—in the

Dave Guyton

Memphis newspaper, Circa 1950

newspaper article. While the date was not captured, the clipping appeared in a Memphis paper around 1950. The estimated date is based on a statement in the text that indicates David Guyton would run for state senator in the 1951 elections. Remarkable is all I can say.

I think of other couples – Florence F. and Walter F. Taylor and May Hall and James E. Buchanan, Lucille Wall and James Travis – the list could go on, even without mentioning the presidents and their wives.

Now Lowrey Memorial Baptist Church is meeting once again as the Blue Mountain Baptist Church, coming full circle as it were. Due to dangerous foundational flaws and other structural liabilities, they assemble no longer in the historic edifice that sits imposingly on the south campus. They wait upon the Lord to give them direction and guidance as they continue to serve Him, under the never-failing Banner of Christ, with Dr. Michael Baker as their under shepherd.

Tracy and Jack Moser are long-time members and faithful servants of Lowrey Church. Speaking not only of Lowrey's rich past, but of Blue Mountain Baptist Church's promising future, Tracy Moser writes:

> I have been a part of Lowrey longer than any other church fellowship in my life. The decision to leave the building was not an easy one, but as our small body of believers has rediscovered, the church is not a building. With that said, Lowrey is a place that holds many special memories including our wedding.
>
> There are certainly some funny memories too, including the time we became pew jumping Baptists! Some squirrels joined our service and we literally experienced the Ray Stevens song (*Mississippi Squirrel Revival* by American country music singer Ray Stevens, released in 1984). Thankfully, we had a couple of youth who were able to creatively capture the visiting squirrels!
>
> We have witnessed lives changed through revival services in that place, as well as countless children running through her halls. Who can forget the leadership of Miss Annie Hendricks with GAs, or the wisdom of Dr. Francis Tyler, along with many other precious saints who have gone on to be with the Lord? The legacy of Lowrey Memorial is a long one. Many Blue Mountain College graduates have attended and served in this church. In many ways, it is quite appropriate that the building belongs to Blue Mountain College now. Students will continue to pass through its halls and be blessed.

And Jack Moser writes:

> In thinking about being a member of Lowrey Memorial Baptist Church for over 30 years, I would say that it has been a time of service, fellowship, and growth, along with periods of struggle. When I first arrived in Blue Mountain, the pastor at the time, Matt Buckles, saw my dad and me moving a washer/dryer into my house. He took off his coat, vest, and tie and proceeded to help us accomplish our mission. That example of service got my attention.
>
> We have had great moments of fellowship from prayer group socials, to potluck meals, to choir practices, to block parties as well as special worship experiences including our wedding. With the longevity of membership, there is no doubt that growth occurred both through those good times and the struggles. Also, during that period, you continue to learn that we are all sinners "saved by grace" as we strive for God's will and purpose.
>
> Another thought came to mind as I was writing these memories. Upon arrival at Blue Mountain College, my direct supervisor, and the Athletic Director at the time, Miss Johnnie Armstrong, was a great mentor and friend. She was a pillar of support for Lowrey Memorial Baptist Church. She loved her church family and considered them her "extended family."
>
> As we move forward as Blue Mountain Baptist Church in a new location, there should be documentation that nothing about this decision was easy. We can honestly say that many prayers were offered, and wisdom sought, as we pondered and continue to ponder God's will for our church. We also can say that God has used the people and not the building over the years to influence our community for Christ. As a church we look forward to seeing how God uses Blue Mountain Baptist Church in the future.

Two other precious members of Lowrey speak to the issue of accepting change with all its challenges. Jean Powell Harrington, BMC Class of 1959, writes:

> I have been part of Lowrey Memorial/Blue Mountain Baptist Church since October 1956 when "join the Church Sunday" was scheduled for BMC students. In those days, the sanctuary was practically filled as students were expected to attend church, wearing hats and gloves. Lowrey Memorial was the church of choice as a car on campus was rare indeed! The Presence of the Lord was surely felt as we entered the almost-silent sanctuary to Mrs. May Hall Buchanan's playing the organ as she did so faithfully for a total of more than 60 years. Looking back, most faculty also lived in Blue Mountain and were actively involved.
>
> Within a span of more than 60 years, fond memories abound. Living near the church, I looked forward to sitting on the porch and listening to the beautiful chimes, especially in the late afternoons. In the early years, Miss Annie Hendricks, along with other Lowrey ladies and BMC students, worked tirelessly with Sunbeams, GAs, and Acteens, providing spiritual leadership (and transportation) especially for the underprivileged children of the community. BMC students who chose to do so were "adopted" by a church family – building relationships between town and college. As a result, students often became very close to their adopted families. Another fond memory is walking with students from Blue Mountain High School, where I was employed, to Lowrey for worship/revival services during the early summer; sadly, such privileges would not be granted today.
>
> As a BMC graduate, in a sense, I had the best of both situations – Sarah Washburn was a dear roommate at BMC and a professor; Johnnie Armstrong, tried to teach me tennis; later I had the privilege of working and worshiping alongside both at Lowrey.

Even though change is inevitable, leaving a building that holds so many precious memories was not easy. True, we regretfully left the building, the usual meeting place, but we didn't leave the Church! Upon leaving, we were reminded anew that we, the people, are the Church. Now we wait for the Lord's direction to move us, in His time, to serve Him from a new physical location. The College will now use the structure to offer students new academic possibilities and allow them to prepare for their God-given calling.

Another long-time member shares her thoughts – heartaches, and all. Von Coombs, who, like me, enjoyed serving as treasurer of Lowrey Memorial Baptist Church for over 20 years, writes:

Lowrey Memorial Baptist Church has been a part of my life for almost 50 years. I have seen many preachers come and go during that time and loved every one of them. For years my husband Butch and I lived across the street from the parsonage and always became good friends with the preacher and his family. I have so many good memories with each family.

A few years ago, the members became concerned that the church building had mold, lead paint and asbestos. After having it assessed for these issues, it was determined unsafe. It broke my heart when I had to leave that beautiful building and I don't think I will ever get past that. Funds are being collected now to build a new church building.

The name has been changed to Blue Mountain Baptist Church.

The good news is that the building has been sold to Blue Mountain College. I look forward to seeing what will happen now. I am sure they have great plans for the building and am so thankful that it will be preserved. Blue Mountain would not be the same without Lowrey Memorial Church.

A WORD ABOUT THE CHURCH FROM
THE PRESIDENT OF
BLUE MOUNTAIN COLLEGE

Dr. Barbara Childers McMillin
From Address to the Alumni Association Annual Meeting
Modena Lowrey Berry Auditorium
Blue Mountain College
August 7, 2021

Let me share good news about Blue Mountain College's plans for the Lowrey Memorial Baptist Church building which the College acquired in June 2021.

A committee consisting of Board members, faculty, staff, alumni, and friends of the College has been formed to study the condition of the facility, to determine what would be required to make it usable, and to propose long-term uses for the building. Committee members include the following: Greg Pirkle, Bob Glover, Harold Wayne Hankins, Sharon Enzor, Stan Irwin, Laura Medley, and Von Coombs.

Dr. Barbara McMillin

The education annex of the property [the part of the building attached on the southwest corner of the original building] will serve as the short-term home for the new Blue Mountain College School of Nursing after some renovations are made.

MISS LOTTIE SHARES SWEET MEMORIES

As Lowrey Memorial Baptist Church was our family's center of worship for so long, with many a thankful, prayerful hour spent under that hallowed roof, I can share what is "good news" from the past. That would be the joys from seeing my two girls, and many others, married in that beautiful sanctuary. Here are some photos from the weddings. They were so lovely. I did not cry until I lay down to sleep.

Wedding of Marjorie Donnell and Charles Easterly in 1950

Wedding of Alice Donnell and Gil Guelker in 1955

Endnotes

[1] W. Carey Hearn, *Lowrey Memorial Baptist Church: The First Hundred Years 1879-1979*, (Fulton, MS: Itawamba County Times, 1979), VII.

Dr. Hearn (1932-1990) was a professor of History and Chairman of the Division of Social Science at Blue Mountain College for many years, having joined the faculty in 1968. His untimely illness and death took him from the classroom where he was beloved by his students, from the community he loved to serve, and from his devoted wife, Betty Holland Hearn (also a favorite faculty member), his son Philip, and daughter Elizabeth. It is from this compilation of church records presented as details in Dr. Hearn's history of Lowrey Memorial Baptist Church that much information for our work of telling the Palmer-Donnell House story was confirmed. We highly recommend it for further reading. The author of this definitive history of Lowrey Memorial Baptist Church was a long-time, active member of Blue Mountain Methodist Church along with his wife and family.

[2] Kenneth Knecht. Lowrey Memorial Baptist Church. July 10, 2016. *https://hillcountryhistory.org/2016/07/10/blue-mountain-lowrey-memorial-baptist-church-1908/*

[3] Hearn, 1.

[4] Ibid, 2.

[5] Ibid, 145.

[6] Ibid, 146.

[7] Ibid, 61.

[8] The History of First Baptist Church, Corinth Mississippi. *http://www.firstbaptistcorinth.org/about-fbc/history*

[9] Hearn, 143.

[10] Ibid.

[11] Hearn, 147.

[12] From a collection of family memorabilia shared by Ellen Guelker Scott, granddaughter of Miss Lottie through Alice.

CHAPTER 7

DRY BONES

The hand of the Lord was on me, and he brought me out
by the Spirit of the Lord and set me in the middle of a valley;
it was full of bones… bones that were very dry.
Ezekiel 37:1-2
The Bible, New International Version

Palmer-Donnell House before renovation

In 1974 my house and I were parted for the first time in over eighty
years. I was devastated. Indeed, I was grateful to be welcomed by my

103

children and enjoyed their care, but I wanted to come home. I knew my house was lonely. I feared my yard would become overgrown with dry, brittle weeds, and that our flowers would wither into hideous, parched brambles. There would be no life…no life. The mental picture of it all broke my heart. I would often lie awake thinking of how broken-hearted my mother would be to see her meandering little brick walkways become choked by invasive weeds and upheaved by harsh, wet, freezing winters. Those were hard days…but happy ones would come.

After two long years of vacancy, the home was sold by my heirs in March of 1976 to James Hale, a retired military paraplegic, who remodeled it to suit his needs. Later, in January 1988, Mr. and Mrs. Paul D. Beaudroux, of Louisiana, bought the home, but never resided there. Once again, the house endured a long period of vacancy. In June 1997, Charles and Margaret "Maggie" Reese bought the home and began a phase of radical renovation. In October 2010, under the leadership of visionary Dr. Bettye Rogers Coward (BMC President 2001-2012), Blue Mountain College purchased the home through the facilitating efforts of Mr. Stan Irwin, and with the financial underwriting of donors, including the Honorable John Norris Palmer, a sixth- generation descendent of the Palmer and Brougher families, native of Corinth, and former Ambassador to Portugal.

Mount Zion Baptist Church on mission

The College began renovation of the house after it was purchased. The work was truly a labor of love led from the onset by Mount Zion Baptist Church of Huntsville, Alabama, and our own Charlotte Bryant Madison (BMC Class of 1969) and her pastor husband, Ron. Their church lovingly embraced this project of beginning the rescue operation for a historical treasure at a strategic time.

In June 2019, the College had a grand celebration marked by the official dedication of the Palmer-Donnell House as the new Alumni House and Welcome Center during the Homecoming on The Hill weekend. President of the College Dr. Barbara Childers McMillin spoke of what this day meant to so many. "If these walls could talk," she said, "they would say to Dr. Bettye Coward 'thank you' for taking the initiative to reclaim us and for believing that we could be restored to our former glory." She went on: "'Thank you, Mr. John N. Palmer,' they would say, 'for regarding your heritage as far back as six generations and honoring all those with your gracious gift which helped the College purchase the house.'"

The walls of my sweet old house would indeed speak out appreciatively, echoing the love of home and family in the now unheard voices of Charles and Allie Palmer, my papa and mama, as well as Lon and me, our sons and daughters – Mac, George, Marjorie, and Alice. From room to room, their whispers would be a grateful "thank you" to those who gave time, talent, financial contributions, and love to make the changes you see. I marvel at the Lord's mercy in bringing to this place so many people with superb abilities – craftsmen, artisans, enthusiastic alums and alumni groups, faithful donors, even our eleven grandchildren, their spouses and children. Energetic members of the Palmer-Donnell House Guild gave and continue to give hours of dedicated service. Their efforts include gathering treasures from near and far to furnish the things that make a house a home, and resolutely guarding the well-being of this home. All these people, in obedience to the Lord's prompting, brought dry bones to life in the walls of this house. These walls do beam with joy.

Yes, Dr. McMillin was right. There would be many happy voices and much applause coming from these walls. Today there are some voices that will be more than a whisper. These voices will speak up with stories about my home and its wonderful journey back from the lonely valley of dry bones. Listen to these voices:

ACCOUNT OF BMC PRESIDENT EMERITA
Dr. Bettye Rogers Coward

By wisdom a house is built, and through understanding
it is established; through knowledge its rooms are filled
with rare and beautiful treasures.
Proverbs 24:3-4
The Bible, New International Version

It was a wet and cold December afternoon when I first rode into the town of Blue Mountain, Mississippi,

Dr. Bettye Coward

and entered the gate to the Blue Mountain College campus. Three buildings caught my attention immediately: Lawrence T. Lowrey Administration Building, a stately campus building which housed most of the administrative and academic functions on campus; Lowrey Memorial Baptist Church, a distinctive structure located on the edge of the campus; and a modest Victorian home (now known as the Palmer-Donnell House) located on private property near the south entrance to the campus. The purpose of the trip was to determine if I wanted to be considered for the presidency of the institution. Obviously, my antennas were up as I tried to assess what I saw and to envision how my experience and skill set might fit with the key leadership role at the College.

Blue Mountain College's historic significance as a Christian educational institution was well established. It had served students faithfully since its founding in 1873, first as a women's college and later adding academic

106

programing for men preparing for Christian ministry. There was a feeling of "town and gown" with the College and community. With the Church and the Palmer-Donnell House located in close proximity to the College, it appeared that they somehow were connected to the College.

Lowrey Memorial Baptist Church was built in 1908 in memory of Mark Perrin Lowrey (1828-1885), a former Confederate General who founded Blue Mountain Female Institute (now Blue Mountain College). Built in the Eclectic/ Colonial Revival style, the Church is "a two-story seven-by-seven-bay brick building with a pyramidal hip-roof, a gable-roofed central section, and a four-story square tower with pinnacled corners."[1] In its original establishment, it provided a place of worship for Blue Mountain College students and the community. To this day, the Church stands as a reminder of the Christian mission of the College.

The Palmer-Donnell House, from its inception, had a long and unique history with Blue Mountain College. Built in 1892 by Charles Frederick Palmer, it was home to the Palmer-Donnell Family who was deeply connected to the College and community. Several members of the family graduated from the College and were active, committed, and influential alumni over the years. Members of the family also served in places of leadership at the College and at Lowrey Church. The house was home to many members of the Palmer-Donnell family. Over time, however, family members moved away, completely vacating the house in late 1974. It became available for purchase in 1976 and passed through several owners until it became available for purchase by the College in 2010.

As I departed the campus that December day, ideas about ways to enhance the physical appearance of property, both on campus and on the surrounding areas, started to permeate my thoughts. Later, I was selected as the president of the College and as I embraced this leadership responsibility, I could only imagine the many opportunities there would be to make a difference. During the weeks and months following that day of seeing the campus for the first time, I continued to reflect on all I had seen and my perception of what "could be."

During my first years at the College, I grew accustomed to seeing the Palmer-Donnell House every day on the drive through the entrance to the campus. The possibilities for its restoration mounted in my thinking. As the Vision for Blue Mountain College was articulated, the College established a master plan to improve and enhance the buildings and grounds necessary to realizing the Vision. Along with the development of a plan for the College campus was the eye toward acquiring property surrounding the campus that would add value to the College and to the town. The quaint Palmer-Donnell Victorian house was in a key location at the entrance of the College campus where the words, "Enter to Grow in Wisdom," were inscribed on the gate. It became clear to me that the house would be an asset to the College as well as to the town. Several reasons for restoring the House emerged.

Improve Perception of the College Campus: Perception of a college campus is shaped, not only by the way the campus looks, but also on the condition and appearance of the properties near the campus. Although the Palmer-Donnell House did not belong to the College at that time, it nonetheless was positioned in such a way that it seemed to be a part of the College. As many older homes and buildings show their age, so did the house. It seemed timely to address the value that this house might bring to the College.

Expand Function of the House: Although the house was small, it was evident that it could provide space for some important functions, thus enhancing its usefulness in serving current constituents. In particular, it could serve to welcome people to the campus and provide space for alumni to gather.

Honor the History of the Institution: The house could certainly honor the history of an era in the life of the College. It could also serve as a reminder to current students, faculty, staff, and the larger community that while institutions change over time, there are core values which remain unchanged through the years. There is much to learn from the past that is relevant today and needs to be preserved. Truth, Knowledge and Virtue, core values of Blue Mountain College, are as relevant today as they were when the institution was founded. This would be an opportunity to affirm the past and anticipate the future.

Visualizing the house in a renovated state was compelling. We were aware, however, that the cost of purchasing the house and the cost of renovating it would be beyond current available resources, especially in light of other pressing needs at the College. As discussions continued, one alumna reminded me of the promise "You have not because you ask not." (James 4:2) and "Ask and you shall receive." (Matthew 7:7) And so, prayer and patience became the mode of operation. Here is how the project unfolded.

Articulate and Communicate the Vision: We knew that it was important for constituents, particularly those whose buy-in would be essential to the successful restoration, to see how it could contribute to the realization of the Vision for the College. Constituents needed to see how the building could look and how it could be useful to the campus today. The historic architecture of the house was compatible with the architecture of buildings on the campus and truly reminiscent of its era. My personal interest in period furniture provided much pleasure in considering aspects of the restoration. Through conversations with alumni, relatives, and residents of the community, there seemed to be sufficient interest in the house to continue pursuing its purchase with hope and faith for its restoration. There was buy-in from a sufficient number of constituents who not only embraced the project, but also became passionate about its success.

Develop Plans for Acquisition of Property: Through providential guidance and evolvement over a long period of time, the house became available for purchase by the College in 2010. There seemed to be no question that the College would follow through with its renovation and upkeep.

Develop Plans for House Restoration: The College Archives were a significant source of information about the house, including photographs. In addition, the College consulted with an architectural firm that was "founded on the beliefs that small towns inspire others

Early work by volunteers

and that family roots can build an ethic that weaves through a profession and that architecture shows the beauty in our history and hope in our future."[2]

Provide Resources to Begin Restoration Process: While there was rejoicing that the College had gained ownership of the house, there was an awareness of the immediate need to secure the necessary resources to actually begin the renovation process, a real challenge. Prior to the beginning of the process, the College had enjoyed the benefits of volunteers in aiding with many projects on campus. We had found that the skills and commitment brought by volunteers could make the difference in whether a project could be completed satisfactorily. Through the connection of one of the College's most committed graduates, Charlotte Bryant Madison, and her husband, Dr. Ron Madison, pastor of Mount Zion Baptist Church in Huntsville, Alabama, a group of volunteers came from that church enthusiastically embracing the long-term project and was able to begin the renovation process, slowly, one step at a time.

Work faced by volunteers

From that point, the College was in a position to move forward with plans to renovate the house and to enhance its use. It was at this time that I retired from the College and was not able to see the project through. However, a team of committed supporters, mainly alumnae, took up the mantle of leadership to complete the project. It was affirming to see how a small group of passionate individuals could determine the success of the project and fully realize its potential. Today, the beautiful white Victorian home, the Palmer-Donnell House, serves as the BMC Alumni House and Welcome Center, extending a warm invitation to those entering the Blue Mountain College campus. It has come full circle, from its inception as an endearing home for a family to the renovation of its structure to extend its use and warmth, thus serving an even larger family.

The individuals who worked on the house during my tenure at Blue Mountain College laid the foundation for success in its eventual renovation and repurposing. It was invigorating to work with them on this project as a part of realizing the Vision for Blue Mountain College. The value and significance of teamwork cannot be overstated, especially among those who volunteered and encouraged others to engage with the College. We were reminded of the ways God accomplishes His work through people. There is no denying that patience is required for realizing a Vision. We know, too, that there is "a time to tear down and a time to build" (Ecclesiastes 3:3, The Bible, New International Version). The renovation of the Palmer-Donnell House is evidence that something can appear dead but can be brought to life if there is Vision, purpose, and commitment. Indeed, it takes the right people at the right time to achieve a Vision. "So we rebuilt the wall...for the people worked with all their heart" (Nehemiah 4:6, The Bible, New International Version).

We really do owe Dr. Bettye Coward a hearty "thank you" and the Lord above much praise for His having brought her to our College and our town. My family is forever grateful for the saving of our beloved home. In 2017, a Guild was formed to follow those who had faithfully worked to develop plans for the renovation of the house. The Guild's purpose is to perpetuate the house's history and support its maintenance through community engagement, education programs and special events. Guild membership is open to individuals who have an interest in preserving history and sustaining this charming home. Information about membership is available by contacting Blue Mountain College at 662.685.4771, extension 131.

One of the Guild officers is Charlotte Bryant Madison (BMC Class of 1969). You will remember her from Mount Zion Church in Huntsville. I remember her as a student at the College. She and Kathie Wessels

Wilson (BMC Class of 1969) were co-chairs of the original Victorian House Committee. Here they both are still serving with such sincere hearts and much zeal to the good of my dear home. I have a letter from Charlotte giving details about the rescue of the Palmer-Donnell House. It is one of the sweetest letters. It delivers such peace and joy. I hold a delightful satisfaction knowing another "Charlotte – Lottie" is in my sweet old home and that she and her friends are watching over it with such passion and dedication. I know in my heart I can trust them with the future of the Palmer-Donnell House.

Yes, once again, our home is alive. Just as the Lord used His obedient servant Ezekiel to perform, through the power of the Holy Spirit an amazing feat in Israel – to bring back life and productivity to dry bones, He was pleased to use the willingness of others to bring back my house. Granting them vision and resolve, He has restored the vitality and viability of my home. The house will serve the College and the community with a new heart and a new purpose.

The Palmer-Donnell House – my home – is a place with a simple but meaningful past that now will be lovingly remembered and appreciated as she goes forward once more serving and enhancing the future. I do rejoice again and again, and in that fond heavenly bliss, dear ones, I now bid you adieu, as I take my leave.

CHARLOTTE'S LETTER

Dear Miss Lottie,

I wonder if you would remember that day in the fall of 1968 when I introduced myself to you on the campus of Blue Mountain College. You were so gracious to extend an invitation to visit in your home there at the edge of the campus – that lovely, white Victorian house that I so longed to explore! As I look back, I wish my motivation had been to get to know you and not just to see your house! But I was a romantic 20-year-old with visions of living in an intriguing older home! Neither of us knew then, as I visited with you at your table, that I would return to your house long after you had departed. Neither did we know that when I returned, it would be to search for and bring back that well-kept, inviting landmark.

Palmer-Donnell House in progress

In fact, it had become an eyesore when a missions team from Mount Zion Baptist Church in Huntsville, Alabama, came in 2012 and decided it would be their next long-term project. I know I am still a romantic because I am writing you this letter which will never see a postmark. There are just so many things to share with you this side of heaven, and I know it will be there that we meet again, Miss Lottie.

You would have loved getting to know the many individuals and families who came in the course of five years to work and help transform that old, decaying structure to its former beauty. These people were mostly members of the church that my husband pastored at that time. They ranged in age from pre-teens to eighty-something-year-olds! Most of the men were skilled workers, not amateurs, with at least two having full-time jobs as respected home builders in the Huntsville metropolitan area. Some team members who lacked construction skills used their gifts in hauling off trash, painting exterior walls and trim, cooking meals for the team, providing cooling snacks (lots of popsicles!) on those hot and humid Mississippi summer days, and being encouragers to those who were

Popsicle break at the Palmer-Donnell project

high up on scaffolding or accomplishing other more technical work.

Like your precious children and grandchildren did, families took vacation weeks and made your home their vacation destination! One family brought their three daughters; another brought two teenaged sons. Grandsons worked alongside their grandfathers and spent a week learning and being mentored by those patient and loving men. Senior adult women who had been serving on church mission teams for years in more

Grandson and grandfather side by side

active construction roles when they were younger now came to take care of feeding the team, and they served some amazing meals. Sometimes these meals were served in the old "Gal-ry" which now houses offices for the College coaches, sometimes in a College-owned house across from campus where the team gathered for refreshing breaks from the heat, and in the last years at the SouthPlex Annex on Highway 15. The SouthPlex had plenty of bedrooms and great space for cooking and serving and eating those lovingly prepared meals. But for those mission team members who eagerly came each year to continue the transformation of your home, their favorite place to be was right there in your yard, under the shade trees, or on the front porch. I'm sure many of them, just as I did back in 1968, were imagining what life must have been like in that old house for the family who were blessed to live there. One lady rescued your spider lilies, replanted them at her home, and now has them ready to bring back when the final landscaping is done. Another saved old square nails and has a package ready to be shared with the Palmer-Donnell House Guild.

The work done between 2012 and 2017 by these friends from Mount Zion Baptist Church was invaluable. They installed new windows and window frames throughout the house. They also designed and installed custom shutters on the west side of the house where guest restrooms were constructed. The original stairs were too narrow and did not meet code requirements. They were removed, and a new staircase expansion was built that included a roomy landing.

Additions to the house after your time (poorly constructed) had to be removed. In addition to the stairwell, other structures were added: kitchen and guest restrooms on the north side of the house and an extended front porch around the east side.

The porch was the focus of many hours of labor, especially by volunteer David Gregory. Mr. Gregory cut and sanded all of the gingerbread trim that had to be

replaced due to rotting. He routed the grooves in the new porch support columns. It was a great shock and sad time for his team and the College family when, on their last work trip to Blue Mountain, Mr. Gregory woke up ill in the night and died before help could arrive. The following year that lovely porch where his skills were so evident was dedicated in his memory and a plaque was placed on the porch wall as a lasting reminder.

A new swing is in place from Elizabeth Buchanan Newcomb in memory of her best friend, your daughter Alice.

The work of new landscaping, new sidewalks and new parking are well on the way to completion.

Miss Lottie, these past few years have given me a second chance to "get to know you" as it were. How thankful I am for that blessing. I am grateful too for the opportunity to stand in your stead – another "Lottie" waving from the front porch, inviting folks in, sharing coffee, and Mother Berry's tea cakes. We will keep the welcome mat out and your dining table ready to host third and fourth generations of your precious family who come to visit Blue Mountain, wait for the train to go through, and savor memories made here.

Please know that your sweet old house continues to stand at 111 Main Street near the Euzelian Gate of the College, ready to warmly welcome all and say, as your mother did so long ago, "Come on up here on this porch and tell us some good news."

Endnotes

[1] Lowrey Memorial Baptist Church history. *https://hillcountryhistory.org/2016/07/10/blue-mountain-lowery-memorial-baptist-church-1908/*

[2] Belinda Stewart Architects, Eupora, MS, January 27, 2021 *https://belindastewartarchitects.com/*

EPILOGUE

From everyone who has been given much, much will be demanded;
and from the one who has been entrusted with much,
much more will be asked.

Luke 12:48 b

The Bible, New International Version

Whatever you may imagine, the story of the Palmer-Donnell House is not over. Many more realities, aspirations and dreams will follow. We invite you to consider the possibilities and engage with us to bring them into focus.

Let's begin with **realities**. *The Palmer-Donnell House is the **Alumni House and Welcome Center** for Blue Mountain College.* While the designation is official, work remains to establish the House as a useful site for alumni to work and relax and for visitors to be welcomed. Funds of $150,000 have been donated from the Estate of Dorothy Wilson Christian as "seed money." While work continues, the House itself is available to host dignitaries and launch campus tours. Completed enhancements will include ground leveling and parking, as well as front terrace and walkways to showcase commemorative bricks.

Dr. Ronald Meeks
Inaugural recipient of
Servanthood Award

In addition, *The Lon and Lottie Palmer Donnell **Servanthood Award*** is a reality that demonstrates a Biblical truth. Since the beginning of the Christian church, believers have identified themselves as servants, just as Jesus made clear that He had not come to be served, but to serve. The award, established by the Palmer-Donnell House Guild, honors genuine servanthood, as consistently lived by Lon and Lottie Palmer Donnell. Their combined years of

121

service to Blue Mountain College, Lowrey Memorial Baptist Church and the Town of Blue Mountain fell just short of 100 years.

The first recipient of The Lon and Lottie Palmer Donnell Servanthood Award is Dr. Ronald Meeks, Chair of Biblical Studies, Director of Church Relations and Ministerial Recruiter at Blue Mountain College. A BMC faculty member for more than 25 years, Dr. Meeks is a well-known and well-loved Bible study leader, speaker and interim pastor throughout the Mid-South region.

Lea Bennett proposed the annual recognition of a student, a faculty/staff member or an alumna/alumnus who demonstrates the servanthood of the Donnells. When presenting the award in November 2021, she said: "Like Professor Alonzo McWilliams Donnell, Dr. Ronald Meeks has served with his whole heart in the instruction and genuine mentoring of young men and women at Blue Mountain College." The Guild is gratified to recognize him as the inaugural recipient of the award, which includes a plaque and gift of $500, and to acknowledge his humble, joyful servant leadership.

The Palmer-Donnell House Guild invites you to participate in the future of the award. You can:

- *Contribute to the award fund for distribution of $500 in future years:* The easiest way to donate is through Blue Mountain College. You may mail a check – with the memo line specifying Palmer Donnell Award fund – to the President's Office at BMC, Box 160, Blue Mountain, MS 38610. Alternatively, you may give online at *www.bmc.edu/giving*

  If you prefer the website option, select "Go" beside "Online Giving" in the list of "Ways to Support BMC." Be sure to select "Palmer-Donnell House" in the field for your donation *AND* under "Additional Information" designate your gift for Palmer Donnell Award fund.

- *Nominate recipients of future awards:* In the summer of each year, the Guild will announce we are accepting nominations in our newsletter and Facebook page. You are encouraged to submit the name and contact information for a current student, current or former faculty/staff member or an alumna/alumnus. Simply say why the person deserves to be recognized for servant leadership.

- *Attend presentations of the award:* The award will be presented in the fall of each year and details about the ceremony will appear in our newsletter and Facebook page.

Now that you've read several references to the Palmer-Donnell House Guild, you may be asking: *What exactly is this Guild?* Another reality, the **Guild** is a group of people united by a single purpose: To perpetuate the Palmer-Donnell House's touchable history and support the House's maintenance through community engagement, educational programs and special events, with a focus on volunteering, hosting and fundraising.

The Guild elects officers to serve a two-year term directing the business of the Guild according to our bylaws. However, the original officers, elected for 2018-2020, continue to serve in 2022 because of the COVID-19 pandemic: President Kathie Wessels Wilson, Class of 1969; Secretary Lea Smith Bennett, Class of 1974; Treasurer Anna Jackson Quinn, Class of 1961; Publicity Chair Charlotte Bryant Madison, Class of 1969; and Preservationist Shelby Carmichael, Class of 2017 *(This office, added in 2022, is exempt from term limits.)*

These colleagues and friends are responsible for writing and publishing this historical memoir about the Palmer-Donnell House and its people. The endeavor drew on numerous published resources and unpublished documents that are cited in the text. The memories of family members and friends were also tapped for valuable narratives and insights. The skills of craftspeople and artisans, both volunteer and compensated, were crucial to the renovation that is central to our story.

Several appendices at the end of this book contain extensive information and photographs. One lists the charter members of the Palmer-Donnell House Guild. We encourage you to engage with us now. If you love Blue Mountain College or the preservation of historic structures, please join! Individuals or couples may join the guild:

- Through a one-time, tax-deductible donation of $250 plus an annual commitment of 10 hours in House-related activities such as guiding tours, maintaining flower beds, performing upkeep or decorating for events.
- Through a one-time, tax-deductible donation of $500 without hands-on commitment.

- Simply send either amount in a check – with the memo line specifying Palmer Donnell House Guild membership – to the President's Office at BMC, Box 160, Blue Mountain, MS 38610. Alternatively, you may join online at *www.bmc.edu/giving*

  If you prefer the website option, select "Go" beside "Online Giving" in the list of "Ways to Support BMC." Be sure to select "Palmer-Donnell House" in the field for your donation *AND* under "Additional Information" designate Palmer Donnell House Guild membership.

A final reality is this: *The Palmer-Donnell* **House is available for use!** If you plan an intimate wedding, a special anniversary or other small event, you should consider the House as your venue. Contact the Director of Alumni Relations at 662-685-4771, extension 119, to select a date and to pay the fee set by Blue Mountain College for the use of campus facilities. Students and campus committees may use the first floor of the house without fee by contacting Alumni Relations.

The Guild will guide future aspirations and dreams for the Palmer-Donnell House. First on our list of **aspirations** is a pair of events we want to see held at the House, beginning when the time is right. We want to host a *Victorian Christmas* with the House decorated for tours, docents in period costumes and music with costumed singers. We also want to host a *Spring Garden Party* with tours and a live drama about the Palmer-Donnell family staged on the lawn.

And what about **dreams**? The Guild truly hopes that we can:

- Launch a speakers bureau and provide compelling audio-visual tools for use with clubs and home-school cooperatives, as well as public school and church groups.
- Develop fee-based summer programs with an opening function, such as Morning Prayer, held at the House before participants disperse to other locations for seminars, retreats, and classes on traditional crafts.
- Design an iron-clad schedule for tours with the long-term goal of being open daily.

And what about concrete **plans**?

- Annual Guild meetings
- Scheduled workday opportunities
- Strategic membership drives

For meeting announcements and updates on the Palmer-Donnell House, see our newsletter. You may join our email list at *www.bmc.edu* Select Alumni, click on Get Involved and scroll down (way down) to Palmer-Donnell House. Select "Join our email list" and submit the form.

For additional copies of this book, go to *www.amazon.com/books*

A WORD FROM THE FAMILY

We love because He first loved us.
I John 4:19
Berean Study Bible

Editor's Note: From the onset the project of telling the story of the Palmer-Donnell House has been a community effort. By community we mean exactly what the Oxford Languages dictionary calls "a feeling of fellowship with others as a result of sharing common attitudes, interests, and goals." The elements of our community include Blue Mountain College whose leadership endorsed and encouraged this endeavor faithfully; the Town of Blue Mountain which remains the peaceful, calm village that is original to our storyline; and the eleven cousins, the grandchildren of Alonzo "Lon" M. Donnell and Charlotte "Lottie" F. Palmer Donnell.[2]

This last section is a word from the family, a rather limited illustration of their whole-hearted partnership in the writing of this book. Of this group of eleven cousins four were asked to represent the family by submitting their thoughts on the project. It may be noted that these representatives are all women. This agrees with the general tenor of our book, written by women. Perhaps this is a not-so-subtle salute to the reality that for 132 years, and certainly during the time that Lon and Lottie Palmer served the College, ours was a school for women. The family remarks are given in the order which coincides with the birth order of the four parents they represent.

The writers of this book wish to express ardent appreciation for the Donnell family cousins and the invaluable help they gave to the project – service given much in the spirit of Proverbs 27:17: As iron sharpens iron, so one person [or family] sharpens another [the BMC family of the Palmer-Donnell Guild]. The Lord is good.

LOVING BECAUSE WE WERE LOVED

Gayle Donnell Westapher, Texas
Daughter of Alonzo McWilliams Donnell Jr.

Reading about the history of the Palmer-Donnell house, Blue Mountain College, and Lowrey Memorial Baptist Church, I cannot help but see the magnificent hand of God at work. The outcome of this book will be a manifestation of the dedication, love, and hard work of so many individuals. This book will help maintain the intentions of Mark Perrin Lowrey in founding Blue Mountain College and preserve the history of

Grandmother's (Charlotte Palmer Donnell's) beautiful home. The history could have easily been overlooked or stored silently for generations with no thought of making the story come to life. The dedication and tireless hours given by the authors of this book have provided my family and generations to come with a beautifully written and vividly told story of our ancestors. This book is a masterpiece. I pray our heirs and those yet born will read and cherish the words as I have, and one day write their own sequel to the Palmer-Donnell House story.

Growing up as a child playing at Grandmother's home, the Palmer-Donnell House, I never imagined that one day this "old house" would have its origin revealed and celebrated. I never imagined that people outside our family would hear the story of my excitement and fears upon being awakened from a deep sleep and swept onto the front porch to watch the roaring train speed past. How could I think that the dining room table where we, as cousins, spent so many hours playing together would be memorialized in a book? It is an honor to have our story told and to further learn the stories of other families in the community, getting a glimpse of the intricate interweaving of the lives of my ancestors and the many people involved with Blue Mountain College.

Oh, how I wish I had known Great Grandmother Palmer (Allie Cossitt) and Granddaddy Donnell (Lon Donnell). Yes, I heard many stories about them, but never had the opportunity to know them. Stories of how Great Grandmother Allie Palmer loved to cook and garden, how she took such particular care of my Daddy (Mac) when he was a young boy, and how much he truly loved her and missed her. To this day, I cherish her creamed corn recipe, a dish shared each Thanksgiving with our family and friends. Through the years I have learned how Granddaddy Donnell was so kind and gentle. I saw those traits in my Aunt Marjorie, Aunt Alice, Uncle George, and, of course, in my own Daddy.

Reading the stories in the book has made me appreciate the special qualities of my Donnell family...my Donnell cousins. As an only child, my cousins are like my siblings. Though we live in different states, we are now closer as a result of the writing of this book. The "Donnell Cousin Coalition," as we call ourselves, has definitely grown closer with each chapter. I am so proud of our family. The members, all different, yet all deeply rooted in their love of God and His church, live life in their own unique ways, but never forget their roots, their ancestors, and most importantly the family's faith in the Lord Jesus.

An old Native American saying rings true today: "Everything we do has an impact on seven generations to come. When we practice good or evil, people are listening. What we say or do will make a mark on future generations." We must continue to ignite and follow our passion for Jesus. Through the pages of this book, I see the impact that a close relationship with our Heavenly Father has had on each generation. I am reminded of the many hours Grandmother Donnell sat in her chair at our home in Austin, Texas, reading her Bible. My prayer is that just as in years past, as our ancestors turned to Him for strength and guidance, that future generations will also do the same, each turning to God for guidance and wisdom.

I encourage others to pay attention to their family history, to make note of their memories and to take pictures of their families. Future generations can benefit from the compilation of these historical pieces into one book – a book that will live forever and be a part of the great family from which you came. I know this book, written about our family, will forever help maintain the memory of Blue Mountain College, the Palmer-Donnell House, and those strong and faithful family members who came before us.

***

Jan Donnell Hockensmith, Missouri
Daughter of George Frederic Donnell

As a child, taking a trip to my father's childhood home filled me with great excitement. I loved the smells of Blue Mountain: English Boxwood around the front porch, the jonquils and hyacinth in bloom, the musty wood of the attic, bacon frying and coffee perking in Great-Grandmother's kitchen. I cherished the times of walking with Great-Grandmother in her garden and greenhouse with the sweet earthy smell from the dirt floor. How lovingly she would hold her flowers and share with me the joy she received from the beauty of God's earth. All of those childhood sensory memories have remained with me today as I too am overwhelmed by the beauty of God's earth.

I eagerly awaited Grandfather to come walking down the hill from

Blue Mountain College after a day of teaching. He was such a kind, jolly man and filled a young girl's heart with love. My father, George, was so much like his father. And I felt so grown up sitting on the front porch in the wicker chairs among the ferns as Grandmother entertained dear southern ladies with tea and cookies. And of course, I, and my brothers, Ron, Fred, and Greg were thrilled to walk to Grandmother's grocery store and get an ice-cold bottle of Coca Cola telling the clerk to charge it to Grandmother's account (with Grandmother's permission, of course). That was big time for a little girl and her brothers who only got cokes when they were in Blue Mountain. Sunday mornings were always a highlight as we attended worship in Lowrey Church, meeting dear saints and singing hymns of love for Jesus.

It was amazing when we heard that the College had purchased our father's childhood home and then pure joy the day we attended the dedication of the Palmer-Donnell House as the Blue Mountain College Alumni House and Welcome Center. How very grateful we were to everyone who had a hand in the restoration of our family's home. We loved the reenactment, by Lea Bennett, of our Grandmother as she greeted us on the front porch. How very clever. So, it was no surprise to hear that Lea and the Palmer-Donnell House Guild officers decided to write a book about the Palmer-Donnell family. These are incredible individuals and we, the George Donnell family, are filled with gratitude for their efforts. We thank them for their diligent research and their kindness in the portrayal of our family.

The Palmer-Donnell descendants were given a very rich inheritance of strong Christian values through our great-grandparents, our grandparents, and our parents. The cousins often comment on how blessed we are to have had such a great foundation of faith in Christ Jesus. We now extend that foundation of faith to our children and grandchildren. Six generations, how marvelous is our heritage! Thanksgiving and praise are given to the Palmer-Donnell House Guild for their vision in sharing our family's walk with Christ through the writing of this book. May all the glory be given to God!

***

Carol Easterly Reynolds, Kentucky
Daughter of Marjorie Graham Donnell Easterly

I am very grateful for my family. Anything good in me comes from my God and from my ancestors. I hope that my life would make them proud. Perhaps the readers of this lineage will grasp a glimpse of the inspiration I have received: a love for knowing Christ, for valuing education, for serving others. Thank you for being interested in a history of my family and the community and college they cherished.

***

Ellen Brougher Guelker Scott, Texas
Daughter of Alice Gayle Donnell Guelker

The love that I have felt for the Palmer-Donnell House has been matched and surpassed by all the participants in the Palmer-Donnell House Guild. While meeting with Lea, Charlotte, and Anna in the newly refurbished home in the fall of 2021, it became evident to me that the passion these women, their spouses and many other collaborators had for the house as well as the family that built and lived in it, was deeply felt. The group has devoted so many hours to preserving the home and its history. I am indebted to them. As a child I felt a deep yearning to be a part of the home. Over the years many members of our family have acknowledged the pull of the history surrounding the family who lived and worked to make the house a home. Many stories of prayerful moments, happy occasions, welcoming new members, and warm homecomings have been handed down to our generation.

My mother, Alice, was the last child born in the home in 1932. She grew up immersed in love and traditions there. After graduating from BMC in 1953, her studies, career and then marriage took her away from Mississippi. However, every chance she could return, she did. Later while my father served an overseas military assignment in 1969, our family bought and renovated the home known then as the parsonage, just two blocks from the Palmer-Donnell House. The parsonage was also located directly across the street from the home our great, great grandfather Dr. Andrew Riley McWilliams lived in while serving as a physician to the college. Grandmother Donnell was still living in her home, and we spent many hours visiting her there. I still remember walking the short distance along the tree-root-broken sidewalk that took us down Main Street. Most vivid are the times my brother, then 7 years old, and I, having just turned 5, were allowed to make the journey on our own. We later learned that phone calls verifying our whereabouts were shared among the adults in the community. Our family waved at passing trains, attended all functions offered at the college, and contributed in many ways to the life of Lowrey Memorial Baptist Church.

During that year in "residence" and the many visits to follow, our family was brought into the loving embrace of the citizens of the community surrounding the Palmer-Donnell home and supported by our own family members living away. These fond memories are irreplaceable. I really appreciate the chapter highlighting the outstanding first ladies of the college. I believe that Alice's ease for hosting and graciousness were learned from these women. I'm sure Mother spent time in Veeve Cockroft Lowrey's home as one of Jean's childhood friends. I always enjoyed being in the company of Mary Frances Landrum Tyler. The description of "her spritely and lovely demeanor" brings back memories of the beautiful talented woman with her light blond hair impeccably arranged in a bun on the top of her head. Martha Huggins Fisher was also a woman of grace. Her older daughter babysat my brother, my sister and me while we were in "residence." Her mother's sweet temperament was displayed in Barbara. She calmly guided us, even though we were a busy bunch of children. We were known to give the "locals" heart attacks as we climbed and hung from the trees bordering our property.

I also appreciate your use of the King James Version for some of the Bible verses quoted. That was definitely Grandmother's favorite version. I have the KJV Bible that she gave me as a child. Grandmother knew many verses and poems by memory. She was very fond of reciting. I do think that elocution should still be a part of basic education! Thank you to the members of the Palmer-Donnell House Guild for your many hours of planning, gathering, organizing work, and overseeing renovations necessary to bring the Palmer-Donnell House into the beautiful condition it is in today. Your dream to make our family home a lasting part of the college's history has come to a happy conclusion. My family and I will be forever grateful to you for your tireless and faithful execution of your restoration vision.

Endnotes

[1] Oxford Languages Dictionary.
https://languages.oup.com/google-dictionary-en/

[2] Again, see Appendix 1 - Descendants

APPENDIX 1

DESCENDANTS OF LON AND LOTTIE DONNELL, 2022

CHILDREN AND SPOUSES

GRANDCHILDREN AND SPOUSES

GREAT-GRANDCHILDREN AND SPOUSES

GREAT-GREAT-GRANDCHILDREN

Alonzo McWilliams "Mac" Donnell Jr., M.D. (1916-1995) m 1947 Lorrayne Vick (1925-2019)

Gayle Donnell m Geoffrey Mark Westapher

Andrea Gayle Armstrong m Ryan Arthur George

Elizabeth Gayle George

George Frederick Donnell (1922-2019) m 1946 Arlene Compton (1920-2014)

Jan Donnell m Phillip Bryant Hockensmith

Brandon Christopher Bridgeforth m Michel Ann Donaldson

Spencer Michael Bridgeforth

Stewart Cameron Bridgeforth

Andrew McWilliams Bridgeforth m Ashley Fontaine Brown

Emma Grace Bridgeforth

Elijah McWilliams Bridgeforth

Isabelle Rose Bridgeforth

Lily Elizabeth Bridgeforth

Ronald Thomas Donnell m Lillian Jean Markowski (1942-2014) m Patricia Ann Hoffman

Katherine Ann Donnell m J. Trevor Jacklin

John Thomas Jacklin

Christopher Mark Donnell m Wendy Sheehan

Quinn Ezra Donnell

Charles Frederick "Fred" Donnell m Charlotte Garton

Jason Matthew Donnell m Amanda Tichner

Logan Mae Donnell

Madelyn Arlene Donnell

Cory McWilliams Donnell

Silas Christopher Smith

Gregory "Greg" Palmer Donnell m Jacquelyn Hamlin

Justin J. Donnell m Nicole King

Kari M. Donnell m Brandon Clevenger

Hadley Gray Clevenger

CHILDREN AND SPOUSES

    GRANDCHILDREN AND SPOUSES

        GREAT-GRANDCHILDREN AND SPOUSES

            GREAT-GREAT-GRANDCHILDREN

Marjorie Graham Donnell (1924-2007) m 1950 Charles Thomas Easterly (1923 – 2003)

    Carol Easterly m Gary Reynolds

        Erin O'Donnell Reynolds

        Hannah Cossitt Reynolds m Kyle Alan Spanik

            Easterly Mae Spanik

            Silas Alan Spanik

    Charles Thomas Easterly Jr.

    Stuart McWilliams Easterly

        Andrew Riley McWilliams Easterly

        Jaclyn Faith Easterly

        Robert Christian Stuart Easterly

Alice Gayle Donnell (1932 – 2007) m 1955 Clarence William "Gil" Guelker (1926 – 2019)

    Mark Guelker m Nancy Tieman Matthews

        Jasmine Jewell Matthews

        Olivia Grace Matthews

    Ellen Brougher Guelker m T. Glenn Scott

        Rachel Maryellen Scott m Micah Davis

        Russell Thomas Scott

        Amy Gayle Scott m John Fletcher

    Elizabeth Ann Guelker m Jeffrey E. Caffey

        Caroline Grace Caffey

        Ethan Luke Caffey

        Emily Kathleen Caffey

APPENDIX 2

THOSE TO WHOM WE OWE SINCERE THANKS
Not a comprehensive list of hundreds for whom we are grateful

President Barbara McMillin

President Emerita Bettye Coward

Jody Hill, President of Memphis Theological Seminary and former BMC VP

Richard Bradford, Founding Partner, The Development Alliance; BMC Friend

Bobby P. Martin

Renovation Team from Mount Zion Baptist Church of Huntsville, Alabama

Stan Irwin

Amy Irwin Thurmond

Tommy Bennett

Manning Graham

Rangel Brothers Construction

Nance Construction

Bryant Painting

Michael Wilson, Wilson's Weaving, Whittling, and Woodwork

Rev. Billy and Renelda Owen

Members of the "Victorian House Committee," predecessor of the Guild

Friends of the Palmer-Donnell House Guild

Donors of furnishings

Guild members who have contributed much encouragement

Alonzo McWilliams Donnell, Jr. MD

Patsy and Harold Wayne Hankins

Emily and Don Newcomb

Former US Ambassador John N. Palmer

Class of 1969

APPENDIX 3

PHOTOS OF RENOVATION PROCESS

APPENDIX 4

PHOTO HIGHLIGHTS OF RENOVATED HOUSE

APPENDIX 5

PHOTOS OF COLLEGE CAMPUS AND COMMUNITY
During Miss Lottie's Lifetime

APPENDIX 6

PALMER-DONNELL HOUSE SPONSORS, GUILD CHARTER MEMBERS AND COMMEMORATIVE BRICK DONORS

SPONSORS

PLATINUM

Alonzo McWilliams Donnell, Jr. MD

Patsy and Harold Wayne Hankins

Emily and Don Newcomb

Former US Ambassador John N. Palmer

Class of 1969

GOLD

Kathie and Ed Wilson

Class of 1968

Class of 1971

Estate of Frances Sue French

SILVER

Jane Clower Bryant

E. Harold Fisher

Clarence Guelker

Imogene Hardon

Mary Ann Harrington

Bobby P. Martin

Elizabeth and Harold Newcomb

Elsie Jackson Norgard

Courtney and Cindy Lowrey Pugh

BRONZE

Laura and Russell Medley

Judith Swanberg

Class of 1961

Class of 1967

Greater Memphis Alumni Chapter

North Alabama Alumni Fellowship

GUILD CHARTER MEMBERS

Emma Ainsworth

Johnnie Armstrong*

Lea and Tommy Bennett

Ashley Ball Berry

Kayce Bragg

Jane Clower Bryant

Barbara Bullock

Von and Butch* Coombs

Cora Davidson

Mac Donnell*

Martha and E. Harold Fisher

Clarence Guelker*

Patsy and Harold Wayne Hankins

Imogene Hardon

Mary Ann Harrington*

Lynne and Timothy Heaven Sr.

Beth Hood

Stan Irwin

Dot and Charles Jackson

Lee Allen Jefcoats

Norma Ruth and Tom Lee

Charlotte and Ron Madison

Ruth Maloy*

Barbara and Bobby* Martin

Frances and Charles Massey

Nancy McDonald

Barbara and Larry McMillin

Brenda McMurray

Laura and Russell Medley

Beverly Moffitt

Rita Newby

Emily and Don Newcomb

Elizabeth and Harold Newcomb

Elsie Jackson Norgard

Renelda and Billy* Owen

John N. Palmer

Cindy Pugh

Courtney Pugh

Denise* and Joe Pugh

Anna Quinn

Carmen and Ty Rains

Ellen Scott

Terry Stanford

Judith Swanberg

Delise Teague

Amy Thurman

Jenetta Waddell

Jamie Johnson Warren

Gayle Donnell Westapher

Kathie and Ed Wilson

*Deceased

148

COMMEMORATIVE BRICK DONORS

Kathy Balof
Betty Bennett
Lea Bennett
Elaine Boling
Donna Brown
Mary Ann Brown
Sherri and Duane Bullard
Audrey Caldwell
Thomas Calhoun
Thomas Callicutt
Marie Claypool
Susan Clements
Leah Crawford
Cora Davidson
Ginger Davis
Mary Dent
George Donnell
Pamela Drake
Cathy Duncan
Nancy Duncan
Joe and Christine Epting
Sandra Ford
Jim Futral
Marva Goodman
Ruth Griffith
Mark Guelker
Lela Hale
Imogene Hardon
Nancy Hart
Lynne Heaven
Gerald and Sherry Hill
Jody Hill
Joy Hill
Jan Hockensmith
Beth Hood
Gerry Hood
Margaret Houpt
Sarah Lynne Huggins
Shelley Jamieson
Lee Allen Jefcoats
Teresa and Ronald Jenkins
Carolyn Joe
Carol Kawasaki

Rita King
Barbara Knight
Mary Langston
Norma Ruth Lee
Heather Linville
Charlotte Madison
Billie Martin
Frances Massey
Johnny Mattox
Kathy McCarthy
Laura Medley
Russell Medley
Ronald Meeks
Beverly Moffitt
Pam Needham
Elsie Norgard
Billie Oakland
Joyce Oglesby
Faye Pepper
Denise Pugh
Anna Jackson Quinn
Barbara Rahrer
Kay Reed
Carol Reynolds
Carolyn Rhodes
Paul Roaten
Jerry Robinson
Ben Sanford
Doris Sanford
Diane Sawyer
Don and Angie Seward
Margaret Smith
Amy Spencer
Terri Stanford
Patty Sullender
Delise Teague
Jamie Warren
Elaine Watson
Betty Watts
Gayle Westapher
Kathie and Ed Wilson
Anna Wright

ABOUT THE AUTHOR

Born in 1949 in the Blackland Prairie of North Central Texas, Lea Smith Bennett grew up, the eldest of five children, in a multi-generational family. Her earliest memories include being lulled to sleep in the lap of her grandfather out in the breezeway swing, hearing laughter and storytelling.

Lea Smith Bennett

"Every person is a treasure trove of stories and experiences that reveal the past in intimate detail, inspire the present with eyewitness accounts, and show the possibilities of the future," Lea explains. "To learn stories and put them in a collection for others to enjoy is a thrill, an indefinable blessing," she says. "That's exactly what this project – *The Year Was 1892* – has been."

Lea, a 1974 graduate of Blue Mountain College, lives with her husband (of 50+ years) Tommy in Ripley, Mississippi. They are the parents of four children, grandparents of seven, and great-grandparents to six.

Considering herself an incorrigible clown, she lists her main hobby is *having fun*; but other activities include Bible study, church work, volunteerism, reading, writing, staying in touch with friends through social media, cooking and entertaining.

Lea concludes: "The Lord has been more than gracious to me and mine, and for that I am profoundly grateful."

Made in the USA
Middletown, DE
27 October 2022

13575366R00091